52 WEEKS
WITH JESUS

J A M E S   M E R R I T T

D0063439

HARVEST HOUSE PUBLISHERS
EUGENE, OREGON

Cover design by Dugan Design Group, Bloomington, Minnesota

Cover photo © jasoncphoto / Fotolia

Published in association with the literary agency of Wolgemuth & Associates, Inc.

52 WEEKS WITH JESUS
Copyright © 2014 by James Merritt
Published by Harvest House Publishers
Eugene, Oregon 97402
www.harvesthousepublishers.com

ISBN 978-0-7369-6101-1 (hardcover)
ISBN 978-0-7369-6502-6 (pbk.)
ISBN 978-0-7369-6103-5 (eBook)

Printed in the United States of America

15 16 17 18 19 20 21 22 23 / ML-JH / 10 9 8 7 6 5 4

"James Merritt's challenge to spend 52 weeks with Jesus is one of both great discipline and great delight. Your passion for Jesus will grow and your life will be transformed through the time you spend in his Word with *52 Weeks with Jesus*."

—**Thom S. Rainer**, president and CEO of LifeWay Christian Resources, author of *I Am a Church Member* and *Autopsy of a Deceased Church*

"In *52 Weeks with Jesus*, James Merritt gifts us with a rich, accessible guide to knowing Jesus more intimately that promises to change the way you see yourself, God, and others. This book will help you drink deeply of the living water, munch on the bread of life, and draw closer to the good shepherd than you ever have before. Read with caution—you'll walk away changed."

—**Margaret Feinberg**, author of *Wonderstruck* and *Fight Back with Joy*

"James Merritt is clear, on point, and writes with authority, wisdom, and compassion. In this book, he confronts the reader page after page with Jesus. Spending time in this book will surprise you, enlighten you, and just might change your life."

—**Russell D. Moore**, president, Ethics and Religious Liberty Commission, Southern Baptist Convention

"Jesus may be the most misunderstood person in history, and part of the reason is that most people have never taken time to actually study his life and teachings, 'Christians' not excluded. It's easy to forget that Jesus was not simply an idea or a topic to debate. Rather, he was a man who turned the world upside down by who he was, the things he said, and what he did. James Merritt's *52 Weeks with Jesus* is an accessible, digestible exploration of Christ's sermons, stories, and miracles. It shatters myths, shakes assumptions, and is littered with surprising insights you've probably never considered. Thank you, Dr. Merritt, for painting a picture of Jesus that is true and textured and as graceful as the first-century Rabbi himself."

—**Tullian Tchividjian**, pastor of Coral Ridge Presbyterian Church and author of *One Way Love*

"*52 Weeks with Jesus* presents dozens of metaphors for Jesus and backs each one up with biblical references, commentaries, meditations, and prayers. I plan to gift it to others often."

—**Leonard Sweet**, Drew University, George Fox University, Sermons.com

"Scripture tells us that blessed is the man who delights in the Word of the Lord and meditates on it day and night. In *52 Weeks with Jesus*, James Merritt provides a believer with a year's worth of meditations on the Word made flesh. His observations on the life, ministry, and Lordship of Jesus are winsome, wise, and well written. Anyone who commits to spending 52 weeks meditating on our Lord will be blessed beyond measure for the effort."

—**Ed Stetzer**, LifeWay Research

"People often approach the biblical narratives of Jesus like a coroner dissecting a corpse, and then wonder why their relationship with Christ is so lifeless. In *52 Weeks with Jesus*, Dr. James Merritt leads readers on a year-long journey to meet, experience, and fall in love with the most important person in history."

—**Andy Stanley**, senior pastor, North Point Ministries

"To know Jesus is to fall madly in love with Jesus. To understand who he is and what he did (and continues to do!) is to be awed and amazed. It will drive you to worship and then service in gratitude for such a great King. James Merritt helps us spend a year in devotional study of the Son of God. I read the book in a single sitting and was once again overwhelmed at the greatness and goodness of my Savior. So, spend a year and soak in this study. I am convinced you will never be the same."

—**Daniel L. Akin**, president, Southeastern Baptist Theological Seminary

"This powerful new book offers a fresh look at Jesus, cutting through centuries of misunderstanding with utter simplicity. James Merritt deeply loves Jesus Christ, and in this book you learn why you should love and follow Jesus, too."

—**Albert Mohler**, president, Southern Baptist Theological Seminary

"Two thousand years ago, an unknown carpenter invited a few extraordinarily ordinary people to be with him. That invitation is still on the table, and has changed the world like none other. Now James Merritt has made it concrete and accessible to ordinary people in our day. I can't think of a better way to spend 52 weeks than to learn from this book how to spend them with Jesus."

—**John Ortberg**, senior pastor, Menlo Park Presbyterian Church

"One of the great ironies of our day is that many people find Jesus boring or—at best—sentimental. No one in the Bible ever found Jesus boring. People either loved him or hated him; flocked to him in admiration or plotted his death. In this helpfully laid out study, James Merritt helps you see the real Jesus—and you'll likely have one of those two reactions. You might be surprised. You might be enraged. But you'll at least know you've encountered the real thing."

—**J.D. Greear**, pastor, The Summit Church

"God's Word transforms us. It transforms me. It transforms you. My co-laborer for the gospel, James Merritt, invites us to invest time daily in God's Word and get to know Jesus. This resource is systematic, compelling, and filled with vivid illustrations. Through it you will find the Scriptures revealing Christ in a fresh way as you spend time with him each day."

—**James MacDonald**, senior pastor, Harvest Bible Chapel, author of *Vertical Church* and *Come Home*

I dedicate this book to the Lord Jesus Christ.
There's nobody like Jesus.
Never has been.
Never will be.

CONTENTS

Section Four: Jesus, the Storyteller

Section Five: Jesus, the Teacher

Section Six: Jesus, the Helper

Foreword

You can't play Bach without expert fingering. But if you focus on the fingering and not the music, you can't play Bach. For at least a century, biblical scholars have focused more on the fingering than the music, and so the strains of a biblical faith have sometimes been hard to hear. James Merritt's *52 Weeks with Jesus* is a brilliant sonata in the limited line of true musicians of the Christian faith.

One of the most prominent virtuosos of the faith among twentieth-century biblical scholars was Paul Sevier Minear, a New Testament scholar who taught at Yale Divinity School. His *Images of the Church in the New Testament*, first published in 1960, portrayed ninety-six images for the church he found in the Second Testament. The book taught me what Jesus was up to in his unique style of communication. Minear was doing brain surgery, or more precisely, soul surgery—he was lifting up metaphors one should be willing to live by and are worth dying for.

This ahead-of-its-time classic book has held pride of place in my arsenal of secret weapons. I've given it as gifts at graduation, ordination, birthdays, promotions. Once, before it was reprinted, I swiped my card and wiped out every copy I could find in the world market.

James Merritt's *52 Weeks with Jesus* is a worthy shelf-mate to Minear's volume. The book presents dozens of metaphors for Jesus and backs each one up with biblical references, commentaries, meditations, and prayers. This book has now been added to my quiver of secret weapons. I plan to gift it to others often.

You will return to this book for its compelling stories and dazzling images. But you will also find in Merritt an immensely allusive writer with wonderfully uplifting messages that come at you like a tarantella—in superb twists and unexpected turns.

Leonard Sweet
Drew University, George Fox University, Sermons.com

Introduction: The One and Only

I fell in love with Jesus in a most unlikely place: a movie theater. Most people who call themselves Christians say their magic moment came in a church service or a spiritual conversation with a friend or perhaps at a tent revival with their feet crunching on sawdust. Not me. I was smitten with Jesus in a small movie theater in rural Georgia, and I've never been the same.

I didn't see many films growing up because Dad didn't care for the cinema. A frugal man, he thought movie tickets were a waste of money, especially when you could just stay home and watch television. But Mom was unlike Dad in one major way: she liked to spend money and looked for excuses to do it.

I had just arrived home from school that Friday afternoon when Mom informed my brother and me that we were "going to the show." I didn't bother to ask what we were going to see. Whether the film featured cowboys or cartoons mattered little to me because I knew Mom would buy us a buttery bucket of popcorn bigger than my head. Besides, growing up in the country, "going to town" and seeing the big city of Gainesville, Georgia, was always a treat.

The Royal Theater was the only one in town, and it showed a single film, usually for two or three weeks. As we approached the building that warm August day, the marquee shouted down at us: "King of Kings." *Was this a medieval action flick with galloping horses and jousting knights?* I hoped so.

After picking up the obligatory popcorn and soda, we searched for seats in a large room that could just as easily have been used as a warehouse for antiques. We walked halfway down the aisle over thread-bare carpet before sinking into three worn-out velvet seats. Then the movie began.

After the opening credits, Jesus showed up on screen, and my eyes widened. I'd heard stories about him since I was in diapers—from his stable birth to his mind-bending miracles to a whole list of sayings in a funny language. I figured he loved me "for the Bible tells me so," but I had never *seen* any of these stories.

Most of the film was interesting enough. Nothing new, earth shat-tering, or extraordinary. But then the crucifixion scene began, and my attention level shot up like a cork on New Year's Eve. The ring of the spikes being hammered into the hands of a man who didn't deserve death stirred anger inside of me. Even my nine-year-old mind recog-nized the disconnect.

Sitting in that darkened theater, my mom unaware, I opened a con-versation with God in my heart. *Why are these Roman soldiers crucifying Jesus? He hasn't done anything wrong. He gave sight to blind people, helped paralyzed people walk again, fed hungry bellies, stood up for the underdog, loved the unlovable, and didn't commit any crimes. Why are they crucify-ing him?*

A response pierced the darkness and penetrated my heart: "*They* are not crucifying him. You are!" Breath was sucked out of my lungs and my stomach turned. What was I to make of such an accusation? I rode to my own defense. *Me? I wasn't there when they crucified Jesus.*

The scene progressed, and I assumed the conversation had ended. I declared myself winner by TKO. But then the voice returned again: "Remember, he died for *your* sins." The voice was right. The Roman sol-diers and spikes weren't the only ones that nailed Jesus to the cross. My sins affixed him there. In some way, I had scourged him, brutalized him, defaced him, humiliated him, spat on him, mocked him, and con-demned him. He died for me, because of me, and instead of me.

And that is the moment I realized it:

There's nobody like Jesus.

I prayed: *Jesus, I believe you died for my sins. I believe you came back from the dead. There is no one else like you. Please forgive me and save me. Amen.*

I sat still for a moment, not sure if I had done anything at all. I didn't feel different. A choir of angels didn't serenade me, no bright lights shone down on my seat, and a deep bass voice didn't shout, "I am God. Welcome into my family." Still, I knew that the boy who was going to walk out of the Royal Theater was not the one who had walked in. I elbowed my mom, and before she could shush me, I whispered, "Momma, I think I just got saved. I just asked Jesus into my heart."

Looking back on this moment, I now realize that I had begun a love affair with a carpenter that day. I fell head over heels for a manger-laid infant. I became obsessed with a water-walking, storm-calming, miracle-working Nazarene. And you know what? I've never gotten over it.

There's nobody like Jesus. And that's why you're holding this book in your hands. Because whether you are a historian, scientist, philosopher, or just an average Joe or Jane, you have to agree that Jesus Christ is one of the most influential humans to ever walk the earth. The secular *Encyclopedia Britannica* devotes more than twenty-one thousand words to Jesus. Major works of art, music, and literature throughout human history have been devoted to telling his story. Even time is divided by his life (BC denotes "before Christ" and AD means "in the year of our Lord"). Though he died in his young thirties, today more than two billion people claim to follow his teachings.

Yale historian Jaroslav Pelikan once wrote, "Regardless of what anyone may personally think or believe about him, Jesus of Nazareth has been the dominant figure in the history of Western Culture for almost twenty centuries."[1]

Yet Jesus's prominence is both a positive and a negative influence among those who follow him. We've heard and seen renderings of him so much of our lives that we think we know him better than we actually do. The life and teachings of Jesus are so rich and deep that those who've devoted their lives to studying the New Testament constantly discover new elements of who he is as they plumb the depths of the biblical record.

As Tim Stafford writes, Jesus has become "deceptively familiar. People think they know all about him, so they never look at him. When they finally do, they are surprised at what they find. Jesus may seem to be a stranger, even though they have grown up in his company."[2]

A few years ago, I began wondering what difference it would make in someone's life if they devoted just one year—a mere fifty-two weeks— to meeting, knowing, and falling in love with Jesus. I decided to test it out. I dived into the Gospels every week for a year. I read books on Jesus. I listened to other messages about Jesus. Every sermon I preached for a year was taken from a Gospel account of Jesus.

As that year progressed, I noticed I was being changed. My passion for Jesus grew, my love for him was stoked, and my eyes were open to new facets of his wonder and beauty and majesty. And all those who had joined me in the endeavor were experiencing the same. That's when I decided to pen this book, because I believe spending one year with Jesus can transform your life. I believe it can help you be a better parent, a more loving spouse, a finer friend, and a more generous, loving, compassionate person.

I fell in love with Jesus sitting in a movie theater nearly a lifetime ago. My prayer is that you will do the same over the next fifty-two weeks.

How to Read This Book

You may have guessed that this book is designed to be consumed over the course of a year. If you choose, you can digest the book more quickly, but the yearlong span is intended to provide time for reflection and to let the material sink in. When you pour rich maple syrup over a stack of pancakes, it takes a few moments for the amber liquid to soak deep down into the flapjack. Similarly, exploring the depths of Jesus Christ is often best done over time.

The book is divided into sections, and each section focuses on a different aspect of who Jesus is. Within each section are chapters—there are fifty-two total, one for every week of the year—and each chapter is divided into five short segments. You can read one segment per day beginning Monday or you can read them all in one sitting and then revisit them throughout the week.

At the beginning of each chapter you'll find Scripture passages to be read and explored every day. At the end you'll discover a prayer and a question for consideration. Journaling as you go may be helpful.

If for some reason you miss a week—you accidentally leave the book on your nightstand and leave for a family vacation or experience an unexpected death of a loved one—don't worry. You can pick back up the following week. My hope is not to add one more obligation to your already packed life, but rather to provide you with a resource that has the power to radically transform it!

Jesus, the Transformer

Birthdays are not unusual—unless the baby happens to be God. We begin our journey with Jesus at a logical place: his lineage and birth. More than a sweet, syrupy Christmas story, Christ's beginning reveals why he should be important to us and why we are important to him.

1

Just Like Us

The Reason You Are Who You Are

What do you do when God falls silent?

That's the question Jewish people were asking during the four hundred years before Jesus's birth.

For centuries God spoke to his people, but when the last prophet, Malachi, wrote his final words and put down his pen, God stopped talking. For nearly half a millennium, they heard neither godly grunt nor heavenly hiccup. Only silence.

When God finally began talking again, the first thing he had someone jot down was a family tree. You may be tempted to skip the genealogy at the front of your New Testament—*Who wants to comb through the names of strangers giving birth to strangers?*—but you dare not.

Why?

Because this family tree is yours!

Imagine if a distant relative told you they had located a family tree that traced your lineage more than two thousand years. You wouldn't wait for a coffee break to read it. No, you'd snatch that sucker up and study it, even if you had to use a vacation day at work.

The genealogies in the Bible are worth our time because they tell stories of how God has moved in the life of your ancestors for millennia and the reason you are who you are. And more to the point of this journey, they tell us a lot about our elder brother, Jesus.

God Oversees the Future

Three names stand out in the rich tapestry of Jesus's genealogy: Abraham, Judah, and David. God promised from the beginning that the Messiah would come through a particular bloodline:

- the family of Abraham (Genesis 22:15-18)
- the tribe of Judah (Genesis 49:8-10)
- the house of David (2 Samuel 7:8-17)

Jesus could *claim* to be the Messiah, but he would soon be dismissed unless he came from the line of King David. All of those "begats" in the Old Testament exist for a reason. God made a promise all the way back to the Garden of Eden that a Messiah would come: *from* a woman (he would be human like us), *via* the family of Abraham (he would be part of God's people), *through* the tribe of Judah and the family of David (he would be both Messiah and King).

Through thirty-nine books of the Old Testament and over four thousand years of history, God was overseeing the future. He was busy keeping his promise, filling out the family tree of Jesus that would result in the birth of the Jewish Messiah and the King: Jesus Christ.

His Tree, My Tree

Every year at Christmastime, the world looks back two thousand years to the birth of a baby. But for more than four thousand years, people living on the other side of that birth looked *forward* to the same event. The birth of Jesus Christ was no accident. It was not the result of chance but of choice.

"So what?" you ask.

Long before we were born, God was overseeing our future as well. We didn't choose our ancestors; God did. God designates our identity, as he did with Jesus, so that we might fit into his plan for the world. In other words, you can know just by your birth and unique identity that God has a special plan for your life.

The next time your world seems to be spinning out of control and you wonder if someone has their hand on the throttle of the train, just read the first verse of the first chapter of the first book of the New Testament. You'll be reminded that Jesus's tree is your tree and that God is in control.

God Overcomes the Past

As Jesus's genealogy unfolds, we discover that because Jeconiah (also known as Coniah) was a wicked king, Jeremiah pronounced a curse on him and his dynasty (Jeremiah 22:24-30). The curse did not mean that Jeconiah would be childless, but rather that his descendants would not inherit the throne of David. But Joseph, the husband of Mary, was a direct descendant of Jeconiah (Matthew 1:12-16). Uh-oh.

As Mary's labor pains begin and our Messiah prepares to take his first breath, we notice a problem in Jesus's past. But—as with us—the past is no barrier for God.

In Matthew's Gospel, the genealogy is paternal going back through Jesus's earthly father, Joseph. In Luke's Gospel, the genealogy is maternal tracing through Jesus's mother, Mary. Jesus's mother was a direct descendant of David, not through the kingly line of Solomon—where the curse of Jeconiah fell—but through another son of David named Nathan (2 Samuel 5:14). One branch of the line of David cuts off at Jeconiah, but another branch descends through Nathan, bypassing this curse.

Legally, Jesus is the son of David through Joseph. Biologically, he is the son of David through Mary.

God can overcome whatever troubles are behind you to achieve the purpose he has set before you.

You're in the Picture

God could have just left Jesus on somebody's doorstep, but instead he did it through the mosaic of ordinary humans. Why did God use all these people in Jesus's family tree?

It has been noted that as few as five points of identification can single out any individual from the billions of other people on this planet: name, street address, city, state, and nation of residence. If someone anywhere in the world were to write those indicators down, they could locate you.

Just as Jesus Christ had certain markers that identified him as the

Messiah, you and I were born with certain signs chosen by God so that we could fit into his plan. God wants our lives to be a masterpiece of his goodness and grace: "For we are God's masterpiece. He has created us anew in Christ Jesus, so we can do the good things planned for us long ago" (Ephesians 2:10 NLT).

Jesus was just like us—born with a past and a history—and we have been made to become like him. God wants you to be a masterpiece of his grace by living for his glory and expressing his goodness to others.

This Week's Prayer: *Lord, thank you for including me in the rich lineage, which has made me a member of your family. Equip me to share your goodness so that more can be called your children.*

This Week's Question: What are the benefits of being included in the mosaic of this particular family tree?

2

A Misfit Among Misfits

This week's Scriptures:

- Matthew 1:1-6
- Genesis 38:1-30
- Joshua 2:1-24
- 2 Samuel 11:1-27
- Ephesians 2:1-10

No-Names and Black Sheep

Most of the people in Matthew's and Luke's genealogies of Jesus are no-names. God promised he would provide a Messiah through Abraham's bloodline, and he did. But when you open up the cedar chest of Jesus's lineage, it is full of dirty laundry. Rather than a roll call of the rich and the famous, parts read like a police lineup.

One thing that would have grabbed the attention of any first-century Jew was the inclusion of women in the list. This was extremely rare since ancients traced lineage through males. And yet Jesus's genealogy in the Gospels includes five females. This sets the tone for justice and equality between the genders that is reinforced throughout Christ's ministry.

But even stranger is the type of women the writers decided to include. If these women had been Rockefellers, Hiltons, or other social royalty, one might expect them to be ancestors of the Son of God. But the women included in the New Testament genealogies are downright scandalous.

Tamar, Rahab, and Bathsheba were the black sheep in the line of Abraham and David. They committed three of the most serious kinds of sexual sins that any ancient could commit: incest, fornication, and adultery. Yet God, in his grace, included them in the family tree of Jesus Christ and used them to produce the world's Savior. God seems to be saying that no one is beyond his grace—a message that Jesus reiterates repeatedly.

God Can Take Us Where We Are

Tamar, the first woman mentioned in the family tree, would have brought a gasp from anyone knowing her history. Her story is one of the most perverse, lurid, sinful events in Scripture.

Jacob's son Judah chose Tamar, a Canaanite girl, to be the wife of his firstborn son, Er. The marriage started rocky and never made it to smooth soil. She was pagan, and he was wicked. Er was so evil that the Bible says God finally killed him.

Here, the story grows complicated. After Er died, the law required that a childless widow should be given to one of her husband's brothers so that she could have children to carry on the family name. One of Er's brothers refused and the other was too young.

Frustrated with being childless, Tamar concocted an evil scheme. She disguised herself as a prostitute, veiled her face, and waited for her father-in-law, Judah, by the side of the road. Judah—willing to sleep with a prostitute—falls for her deception. Out of this relationship, twin sons were conceived. Perez, who was born first, became an ancestor of Jesus Christ.

God weaves this cord into the tapestry of Jesus's family tree to make a point: No one is beyond grace. God can take you where you are and fit you into his plan and his purpose.

God Can Change What We Are

Rahab was a prostitute by trade. She was what one Bible scholar called "the Madame of Jericho." Outside of Matthew's genealogy, every time Rahab is mentioned in Scripture, she is referred to as "Rahab the prostitute." She was also a Canaanite—a mortal enemy of Israel who worshiped a false god. (The Canaanites were to Israel what al-Qaeda is to the United States.) Yet, God also decides to include her in the family tree.

After forty years of wandering in the wilderness, the Israelites prepared to enter the Promised Land. Joshua had sent spies to scout out the city of Jericho. When they came upon Rahab, they asked her to hide them. She tucked them away in her home.

When the enemy came looking for them, Rahab lied to protect them. Knowing the Israelites would destroy the city, she bargained with the spies to save her family. They agreed not to take her life or her family's if she would hang a scarlet thread from the window of her house, so her family could be identified and spared.

Rahab not only risked her life to protect God's people, she abandoned the gods of the Canaanites for the true God. This professional prostitute ended up becoming the great-great-grandmother of David and ancestor of Jesus. Mark up another point for grace.

God Can Use Who We Are

When David gazed across the city from his rooftop, he noticed the beautiful Bathsheba bathing. Enamored, he sent his servants to fetch her. Their secret one-night stand wouldn't remain secret for long, because Bathsheba became pregnant and her husband was away at war. As a result, David ended up devising a scheme to kill her husband so he could marry her.

Bathsheba didn't have a choice when the king called for her—she had to go. But because of the culture, she was an object of shame as an adulteress. To add to the tangled mess, she married her husband's murderer. This is a story that is as complicated and despicable as any in the Bible (or Hollywood, for that matter!).

Yet somewhere, someway, somehow God chose to use Bathsheba. Even though the first baby died, Bathsheba conceived again and bore a son named Solomon, who became the next link in the divine chain of God's Son, Jesus.

God can take your complicated messes and use them for good.

An Unlikely Mosaic

You would have expected the family tree of Jesus to be a Hall of Fame—filled with heroes and sages. But some parts of it feel a bit like a Hall of Shame instead. Jesus's family line was populated with Gentiles, fornicators, adulteresses, prostitutes, liars, wicked kings, and other rascals.

It's actually fitting that God would use this group of misfits to give us a Savior. Because the Savior, Jesus, would be a misfit himself. No, he didn't sin. But he would shatter preconceptions again and again. Jesus refused to fit the mold people had fashioned for the Messiah, shocking the masses at every turn. At the end of a long line of misfits, we encounter a "misfit Messiah."

Through Jesus's family tree, God puts his grace on display. God is reminding us that he can do for us what we cannot do for ourselves: pick up broken pieces and put them together, take broken lives and make them whole, gather broken hopes and make them reality. That is the message of Jesus's family tree.

This Week's Prayer: *Lord, I thank you that no one is beyond your supernatural grace and that you choose to work through imperfect human vessels. Use me to your glory.*

This Week's Question: What are the broken places in *your life* that God has chosen to work through?

3

A Messy Messiah

This week's Scriptures:

- Ruth 1
- Ruth 2
- Ruth 3
- Ruth 4
- Matthew 22:41-46

Of Royal Lineage

The actress Brooke Shields has quite an impressive family mosaic. Hanging from her family tree are the likes of Charlemagne, El Cid, William the Conqueror, the royal houses of virtually every European country, and five popes—prior to the twelfth-century imposition of celibacy!

She's not unique, though.

Experts say that even without a *documented* connection to some notable ancestor, the odds are virtually 100 percent that every person on earth is descended from one royal person or another.[3] It works the other way as well. Anyone who had children more than a few hundred years ago is likely to have millions of descendants today, quite a few of them famous.

You may be a royal blueblood right now and not even know it. You may have the blood of some king or queen flowing through your veins.

In the genealogy of Jesus, God demonstrates that anyone can become a part of the greatest royal family of all—the family of not just *a* king, but *the* King of kings.

Who would *not* want to be a part of God's family? Who would not want to have a seat at his table? Who would not want to be a piece in his mosaic? God became a part of the human family so that we could become a part of his heavenly family.

Everyone Is Invited to God's Family

Matthew was a Jewish author writing to a Jewish audience about a Jewish Messiah. Jews, rabbis, and Hebrew scholars would have been extremely intrigued reading about the lineage and the family tree of this man named Jesus Christ.

But what if you weren't Jewish? What if you were a Gentile?

For thousands of years, Gentiles were on the outside looking in. So were a Gentile to read this extremely Jewish genealogy, he might think, *So what? This doesn't help me. I'm a Gentile.* That a woman named Ruth appears in Jesus's genealogy, though, *may* help.

Ruth was a Gentile, a Moabite, a tribe of people who were descended from a cursed race and whose existence was repugnant to the Jewish people. The Moabites fought Israel for many generations and were their mortal enemies.

So here is a knot in the family tree of Jesus.

Ruth had married one of the two sons of a woman named Naomi, but Naomi's husband and both her sons died. When they did, Naomi decided to leave the country of Moab and go back to her native land of Israel. One daughter-in-law chose to remain in Moab, but Ruth chose to stay with her mother-in-law, forsaking her heritage to follow the God of Abraham, Isaac, and Jacob. And God rewarded her faith. Ruth remarried a close relative of Naomi, becoming the great-grandmother of King David and an ancestor of the Lord Jesus Christ.

Everyone Is Included in God's Love

Joseph was not the biological father of Jesus. And so that raises the question that Jesus himself asked the Pharisees in Matthew 22, "What do you think about the Christ? Whose son is he?"(Matthew 22:41-42). Jesus was telling the Pharisees that they should be wondering, "Who's your daddy?"

The virgin Mary conceived the baby named Jesus by the Holy Spirit of God. Both the virginity of Mary and the activity of the Holy Spirit were necessary so that God could become a part of the human family.

There were other ways that God could have accomplished his will.

God could have created Jesus as a complete human being in heaven and dropped him on the doorstep of planet Earth without the benefit of any human parent. But then, nobody would have believed that he was fully human. On the other hand, God could have had Jesus come into the world with two human parents, and somehow miraculously preserved his divine nature, but nobody would have believed that he was fully God.

God in his wisdom saw to it that Jesus would be conceived by the Holy Spirit and born of a woman so that both his full deity and his full humanity would be evident from the moment of his conception to the time of his birth. As a human he would be one of us; as God he would love all of us.

Everyone Is Important to God's Heart

Matthew's genealogy goes all the way back to Abraham, but he stops, because he is talking to the Jews. But Luke, who is also a Gentile, goes all the way back to Adam: "the son of Enos, the son of Seth, the son of Adam, the son of God" (Luke 3:38).

While he was on this earth, Jesus Christ was fully human, just like you and just like me. He was tempted, hated, persecuted, beaten, hungry, thirsty, and brokenhearted just like you and just like me.

As striking as that is, the central point of Luke's genealogy is the fact that it *ends* in God. Do you see the last four words, "the son of God"? That ending is one of a kind. There is no parallel in the Old Testament or in any other ancient text for a genealogy that begins or ends with the name of God.

Yes, Jesus is the son of Adam. He is a human being; but he is *also* the Son of God. He became a part of our human family so that we could become a part of his heavenly family:

Christ, the Son of God
Became a son of Adam
That we, sons of Adam,
Might become sons of God.

Pieces of the Mosaic

When Jesus Christ became a part of the mosaic that we find in Matthew 1 and Luke 3, when he became a part of a family tree, he was saying to every person who would ever become a part of the human race, "I love you. I want to be your Savior. I want to save you from your sins. You are important to my heart." Not only did Jesus become a part of the human family, but this patchwork mosaic tells us that *we* can become a part of his *heavenly* family.

You and I get into the human family, the *Adam* family, the same way Jesus did: by physical, biological birth. But to get into the *Jesus* family, we have to experience a spiritual birth. The first time you are born, you are born into the family of Adam; but when you are born again, you are born into the family of Jesus Christ.

The New Testament is the story of a family: the family of Jesus. God became a part of our family so that we could become a part of his. And just as God used two ordinary women named Ruth and Mary to make a lasting impact on the world, God can use you to make a lasting impression on others by your living for him and loving him and doing his will.

This Week's Prayer: *Lord, thank you for becoming part of the human family so that I could become a part of your heavenly family. Teach me how to live for you, love you, and do your will.*

This Week's Question: Who do you know who's not yet a part of God's family who could become a part of this family tree?

Section Two

Jesus, the Answer

Like Hansel and Gretel, Jesus drops bread crumbs along the path to knowing him. He offers us symbols, images, pictures, and clues to remind us that he is more than skin and bones. Though he is human, he is not like your next-door neighbor or cranky landlord. He is far different—better—than they. Jesus uses seven "I am" statements in the Gospel of John to share the intricate folds of his personality and identity. They help us understand not only *who* he is but also *what* he wants to be for us.

4

Bread for the Journey

This week's Scriptures:

- John 6:22-40
- John 6:40-59
- Exodus 16:1-21

- Nehemiah 9:9-21
- Psalm 78:17-25

Hungry People

Who am I?

This is the question Jesus answers through seven statements found only one place in the four Gospels.

Jesus begins: "I am the bread of life" (John 6:35,48). The metaphor is rich, even for modern readers. Travel to almost any country in the world and sit in any restaurant and you will likely find some type of bread on the menu. Not every restaurant serves steaks or seafood. Unfortunately, most restaurants don't offer chili dogs, fried chicken, and onion rings (some of my favorites), but almost all serve bread. Bread is a staple of life since the beginning of time.

"What food is to your body I am to your soul," Jesus said.

Bread is one thing most humans share in common. If poor people don't have anything else, they probably have bread. Rich people who have everything else will usually also eat bread. Bread is not a food that belongs to a particular region or a particular country. It comes in all shapes and sizes. In South America, it may be a tortilla. In New York, a bagel. In Georgia, a biscuit. If you travel to Ethiopia, you'll find injera.

In one simple statement, Jesus reminds us that he is sustenance for all people in all places at all times.

Jesus the Feeder

Jesus had just finished feeding five thousand people with a few loaves of bread and a few fish. He and his disciples had left the crowds and gone across the Sea of Galilee to a place where they thought they could get some rest, but instead the crowds followed them. Jesus knew exactly why they came.

> Jesus answered them, "Truly, truly, I say to you, you are seeking me, not because you saw signs, but because you ate your fill of the loaves" (John 6:26).

Jesus not only knows *what* we do, but he always knows *why* we do it. Jesus wants us to follow him for the right reasons, and this crowd wasn't. They thought they had struck gold with Jesus. He was going to be their bread maker and their fish baker. He was not just a Messiah but a meal ticket. Not just the Christ but a cosmic cook.

While Jesus wanted to provide for their physical needs, he also had something else in mind.

Look for the Spiritual, Not the Material

The crowds saw someone in Jesus who could put a steak on every table and meet every physical necessity they had. But in their obsession with the material, they overlooked the spiritual. Jesus challenged them to quit working for the stuff that won't last and start focusing on the things that will. Then someone asked a great question:

> "What must we do, to be doing the works of God?" Jesus answered them, "This is the work of God, that you believe in him whom he has sent" (John 6:28-29).

They don't like that answer.

> So they said to him, "Then what sign do you do, that we may see and believe you? What work do you perform? Our fathers ate the manna in the wilderness; as it is written, 'He gave them bread from heaven to eat'" (6:30-31).

They were saying, "Moses fed the people of Israel every day with manna from heaven. Why can't you at least be equal with Moses and do what he did?" Jesus wanted to be their Savior, but they wanted a sugar daddy.

Live for the Eternal, Not the Temporal

Do you know why the physical and the material can bring only temporary satisfaction? *Stuff* is temporal, but your soul is eternal. By its nature, the temporal can never bring security, significance, and satisfaction to the eternal. No matter how much money you have, you will always want more.

Think about your typical Christmas dinner. You sit down and eat until your belly can't contain another morsel. Then, you get up and say, "I'm so stuffed I don't care if I ever eat anything again." You are totally satisfied for about three hours, and then you return to the refrigerator looking for leftovers.

Hunger is something that God has built into the human body to remind us to eat, because we'll die without food. There is a spiritual hunger in the human heart and an eternal hunger in the human soul that can never be satisfied with anything other than Jesus Christ, the Bread of Life.

The world wants to satisfy your body. Jesus wants to also satisfy your heart. The world wants you to focus on what will eventually die—your body. Jesus wants you to focus on what is going to live forever—your soul.

Bread that Satisfies

Think about how bread is made. The process begins when grain is planted in a field. Upon ripening, it must be cut down, ground into flour, and made into dough. Then, before it can become bread, it has to pass through the fire of an oven.

Jesus was planted as a seed in the womb of a virgin. He was born into this world and grew up completely sinless. And when he was ripe, at the height of his ministry, he was cut down, put through the fire of the oven of God's wrath in the shape of a cross. But he came out of an empty tomb as the finished Bread of Life.

After World War II, Europe was overwhelmed with a number of hungry, homeless children who had been orphaned by the conflict. These children were placed in large camps where they received sufficient food and care. But the caregivers noticed the children did not sleep well at night. They were anxious and fearful and restless.

The caregivers were stumped until a psychologist formulated a solution. He instructed the caregivers to give each child a piece of bread, not to eat, but to hold after they were put to bed.

The results astounded all. The children slept through the night because they knew they would have food the next day. Holding bread gave them a sense of security (they were safe), significance (somebody cared about them), and satisfaction (there will be more bread tomorrow). Those things are what those children needed—and what every person needs.

We are all born with this hunger, but our growling souls can be satisfied only by the Bread of Life.

This Week's Prayer: *Lord, Giver of all good gifts, teach me to hunger for bread that truly satisfies.*

This Week's Question: Are there other appetites and cravings in your life today that quench your hunger for what is spiritual and eternal?

Light in a Dark Place

In Deep Darkness

Years ago, my wife and I traveled to Kentucky where I went to seminary and decided to stop and tour Mammoth Cave. The trip marked my first and only time ever to be in a cavern like this, and I'll never forget it. We descended deep into the cave, and then without warning the guide turned off his flashlight.

Have you ever heard the term *achluophobia*? It is the fear of darkness. If I didn't have it before I went into the cave, I think I was afflicted with it after I emerged.

Being in complete darkness is unnerving. It induces a sense of helplessness. And yet physical darkness is nothing compared to emotional, relational, and spiritual darkness. When you are in the dark and can't see your way through, can't find your way out, Jesus lights the torch.

> "I am the light of the world. Whoever follows me will not walk
> in darkness, but will have the light of life" (John 8:12).

Light Is Absolutely Essential

Light is one of the things we often take for granted. Light is essential to life, and we could not live without it. Plants are necessary for the existence of mankind. The entire human species and all animal life are dependent on plants for survival. Plants provide all the essential amino acids and most of the vitamins necessary for health through a light process known as photosynthesis. Plants also produce the oxygen that we need to breathe. And plants must have *light* to grow.

What is true in the physical world is true in the spiritual world. Physical life is impossible without physical light, and spiritual life is impossible without spiritual light.

When the light went out in Mammoth Cave that day, those of us there were in complete darkness and couldn't see. However, one person not only knew the way out, he had something priceless in his possession: a light.

A Land of Deep Darkness

Have you ever felt like you were in darkness you could not escape?

- "My girlfriend left me for another guy."
- "I'm probably headed toward divorce. My husband has been cheating on me with prostitutes."
- "I'm depressed and cry for no reason. When will the blues go away?"
- "I am wrestling a terrible illness, and I'm basically a shut-in. I am in a dark place and need help."

What do you do when the sun doesn't seem to rise? How do you dispel the darkness? If you're stumped, ask yourself, "If I wanted to get rid of darkness in a room, how would I do it?" Would you sit down on a couch and feel sorry for yourself? Would you take a broom and try to sweep the darkness away? Would you try to shovel or vacuum the darkness out?

There is only one solution to such a quandary: turn on the light. Darkness runs for the hills when light comes. And Jesus is the light that banishes spiritual and emotional darkness.

Jesus didn't say he is *a* light, one among many, but rather *the* light. He didn't say he is a light just *for some*, but the light *of the world*. And when life is at its darkest, Jesus is at his brightest.

If you are living in darkness, you're invited to step into the light.

Come into the Light

Jesus makes an incredible promise that the moment you come to him, surrender to him, you will never walk in darkness again. How can Jesus be so confident? Because even though Jesus called himself "the light of the world," he also called us the same thing, saying to his disciples in Matthew 5:14, "You are the light of the world."

Of the seven things that Jesus calls himself, this is the only title that he also gives us. If you are a follower of Jesus Christ, you should also be light amidst the darkness. Your job is to let Jesus shine in you and through you so that those living in the dark will find the light as well.

That's why it's not enough just to shine.

Light is useful only when it encounters the darkness. The place to shine your light and show your light and share your light is not *inside* the church, but *outside* the church. Jesus tells us to do what he did: go find dark places and start shining.

When you're in the darkness, Jesus shines his light. But if you are living in the light, Jesus calls you to shine into the darkness.

We Must Shine the Light to People in Dark Places

You don't have to ask people to look at you when you turn on a light in a dark room. Their heads will turn instinctively.

- You play sports, and you begin praying for and with your teammates. You are a light in the darkness.

- You live in a neighborhood filled with unbelievers and begin performing acts of service for others in Jesus's name. You are a light in the darkness.

- You are the conspicuous Christian in your office, displaying virtue in an atmosphere of selfishness. You are a light in the darkness.

Jesus called us to find people in dark places and to move toward those who need him. As it turns out, escaping from darkness is as easy as turning on the light.

This Week's Prayer: *Lord, shine into my heart and my life. And where there is darkness, let me bear your light to the ones you love.*

This Week's Question: Are you living in the darkness or in the light? Where is Jesus calling you?

6

An Open Door

This week's Scriptures:

- John 10:1-10
- Isaiah 12:1-6
- Hebrews 13:5-6

- John 1:9-12
- Colossians 3:1-4

A Different Kind of Door

When Jesus said, "I am the door," he wasn't describing the kind with metal knobs, squeaky hinges, or shiny keys.

> "Truly, truly, I say to you, I am the door of the sheep. All who came before me are thieves and robbers, but the sheep did not listen to them. I am the door. If anyone enters by me, he will be saved and will go in and out and find pasture" (John 10:7-9).

First-century listeners knew exactly what Jesus meant, but our modern ears easily miss it. In Israel, there were two kinds of sheepfolds. One was near a village or a town, and it was an enclosure for the sheep of all the shepherds. The owners of the sheep would pool their resources and hire someone to guard their flocks.

The other kind of sheepfold was out in the hills away from any village. On three sides, rocks would be piled about a foot high, and there would be a small opening about five- or six-feet wide where the sheep would enter at night. The shepherd would lie down in front of that opening and become *the door* for the flock. Nothing could go in or out unless the shepherd allowed it.

As the door, the shepherd gave sheep the same three things we saw earlier that every one of us crave. He gave the sheep *security*—they knew they were safe as long as the shepherd was at the entrance. He gave the sheep *significance*—they knew they mattered to the shepherd and he cared for them. He gave the sheep *satisfaction*—because he provided them with food and water.

The Door of Security

The shepherd was responsible for making sure the sheep felt secure. Wolves and robbers came at night to either eat or steal the sheep. The flock could rest only if they knew that their shepherd was protecting them with his life.

That is what Jesus means when he says, "If anyone enters by me, he will be saved and go in and out..." (John 10:9). Timid, frightened sheep would stay in the fold day and night and never go out to pasture due to fear. The careless, overconfident sheep remained in the pasture all day and, ignoring the danger, never returned to the fold. The shepherd made sure the sheep knew coming in and going out was safe.

Jesus reminds us that we all need his presence in our lives. Only he can provide the safety we desire.

Maybe you identify with the fearful or careless sheep. You feel as if you've walked through your share of wrong doors or have never left the pen. It's never too late to walk through the right door. The door stays open, and you can enter anytime you wish, knowing that Jesus himself will protect and provide for you.

The Door of Significance

One of my favorite films is *Braveheart*. In a gripping scene, William Wallace, the hero, announces, "Every man dies...but not every man lives." You haven't lived until you have met, surrendered to, trusted, loved, and made Jesus your friend. When you come to Jesus, you exit a life of meaninglessness and you enter a life of meaningfulness.

"The thief comes only to steal and kill and destroy," Jesus said (John 10:10a). The thief is the one who holds open the wrong door and invites you to walk through it. If you walk through the door of greed, lust, jealously, or selfishness, it will suck joy and peace out of your life. It will rob you of significance and will leave you totally unsatisfied.

When you walk through the door named Jesus, everything changes. He goes on to say, "I came that they may have life and have it abundantly" (John 10:10b).

Jesus put you here to live for him. He provides the purpose you've been pining for.

The Door of Satisfaction

Jesus extends the sheep metaphor by saying that the one who enters through the door he provides "will go in and out and find pasture" (John 10:9).

It doesn't take a lot to satisfy sheep. They are one of the simplest and easiest creatures to care for. Give them green grass to eat and clean water to drink and you will have a happy flock.

Every morning, the shepherd would take the sheep out of the fold, lead them to green pastures where they could feed, eat, and rest. In the evening, when the shepherd led the flock back to the fold, he gave each of them a cool drink of water. Then, as they passed back into the fold, he would check to see if they had any cuts or unwanted bugs or insects, and he would apply medication, usually oil. He would also check to see if they'd picked up any thorns or burs, and he would clean their coats. His job was to make sure the sheep were satisfied when they were up in the daytime and cared for and safe when they went down for the night.

Jesus is the door that *truly* satisfies.

Searching for the Door

Years ago, UCLA psychologist James Coleman wrote, "As the modern day person struggles with the baffling question of his own existence…science falls short of providing full answers…it can tell how, but not why." Coleman adds, "Despite their fine automobiles, well-stocked refrigerators, and other material possessions and comforts, the meaning of life seems to be evading them. They are suffering from existential anxiety—deep concern about finding values which enable them to live satisfying, fulfilling, meaningful, and [significant] lives."[4]

People go through life trying to find the doors of security, significance, and satisfaction, but they never do. Be honest with yourself. Are you secure in who you are, what you have, where you are going? Do you feel significant? Are you giving your life to things that matter and make a difference? Are you satisfied? Is there a settled peace in your heart when you go to bed and rise in the morning?

If you are honest and transparent enough to respond no, here are four words Jesus said that you need to hear: "I am the door" (John 10:9).

This Week's Prayer: *Lord, thank you that you are the Door to abundant and eternal life, and that you have invited me to enter in. I trust you to meet my deepest needs.*

This Week's Question: Have you exited the door of a meaningless life and entered into the door to a life of security, significance, and satisfaction?

7

The Good Life

This week's Scriptures:

- John 10:10-18
- Psalm 23
- Isaiah 40:9-11

- Ezekiel 37:24-28
- Micah 5:1-5

An Unfortunate Comparison

Jesus doesn't just use the shepherd metaphor when he refers to himself as the door. Over and over in the Bible we are compared to sheep. Some people think it's heartwarming. But I hate to tell you, it's not flattering.

You won't find a dumber animal than sheep.

Dogs and cats can be trained, but you'll never go to a circus and buy a ticket to see a trained sheep. They have poor eyesight. They have no common sense. Left to their own, they'll walk into a stream and drown. Sheep are prone even to walk off a cliff and plummet to their death.

We are different from sheep in at least one way: we worry. Sheep are too dumb even to worry that they can't take care of themselves. But we do. Especially when we confront situations that we can't handle or we're put into circumstances we can't manage.

You either have or will have worries you can't resolve. The anxiety of a marriage that's seemingly on the rocks or the frustration of a teenager who's headed down the wrong path. The worry of an illness that may not get better or a bank account that's falling deeper into the red.

The best life is one where you face your deepest fears, darkest places, and greatest worries with *faith* rather than fear. When you understand you're a helpless sheep, you also understand that Jesus is the Good Shepherd (John 10:11). And that leads to a powerful truth: sheep need not fear when the Good Shepherd is near.

Cowboy or Shepherd?

Do you know the difference between a cowboy and a shepherd? A cowboy *drives* cattle but a shepherd *leads* sheep. When Jesus says, "The thief comes only to steal and kill and destroy" (John 10:10), he is referring to Satan. Do you ever wonder if you're headed in the right direction with your life or with the decision you're about to make? Remember that the Shepherd will guide you to the right places, but Satan will drive you to the wrong places.

A group of tourists visiting the Holy Land passed by a flock of sheep being driven into town. The tourists were taking pictures and one of them asked the guide, "I thought the shepherd led the sheep from the front. Why is he in the back?" The guide said, "That's not the shepherd, that's the butcher."

That's the position Satan will always take in your life. Driving you, shoving you from the rear with reminders of your past, filling you with guilt and anxiety, riddling you with fear and uncertainties in the present, whispering to you worries about the future. But Jesus will make you lie down in green pastures. He'll lead you beside still waters.

Protector, Not Preventer

I recently had dinner with one of my congressmen in Washington, DC. He lives in an area where a tornado had just devastated hundreds of homes. He showed me on his cell phone one of the most incredible pictures I've ever seen. It was a photograph of a tornado that looked as if it were right behind the elementary school where two of his children attend. The twister miraculously went behind the school and did little damage. But he remarked about the helpless feeling that picture gave him knowing he could not have done anything to protect his children that day.

We are all helpless against the unexpected tornados in our lives. We can't predict or fully safeguard against a drunk driver, deranged killer, determined terrorist, or deserting spouse. Just like sheep, we need a shepherd who can get us where we need to be.

Shepherds cannot keep sheep from difficulty. Wolves and bears want to devour the sheep. Bad weather threatens the flock. Ticks, fleas, and other parasites can sicken and weaken them. The shepherd cannot prevent sheep from coming into contact with bears or wolves, but the shepherd can protect the sheep when they do.

Jesus does not guard us *from* difficulty; he guards us *in* difficulty.

Known by Name

I'm fascinated at how Jesus looked at people. We tend to see nameless faces, bland personalities, a list of hang-ups or hiccups. But when Jesus stared into a set of eyes, he really *saw* the person behind them. Jesus explained,

> "I am the good shepherd. I know my own and my own know
> me, just as the Father knows me and I know the Father; and I
> lay down my life for the sheep" (John 10:14-15).

"To know" means much more than just to be able to identify a person by name. In the Bible, "to know" involves intimacy, the deepest understanding of another person. Shepherds did not know their flock just as a whole; they knew each sheep individually.

They gave each sheep a name and could call an individual sheep out of the fold. But those shepherds also knew the nature of each one. They knew which were prone to wander, the ones that were stubborn, and those that tended to get into trouble. The Good Shepherd knows the needs of the sheep and knows exactly how, when, and where to meet those needs.

Guaranteed Security

What do you think the price would be for a car or plane or train that was guaranteed to withstand any accident? How much would someone pay for a ship guaranteed never to sink under any circumstances? Having a shepherd to guard you and guide you not only in this life but all the way to an eternity is of infinite worth. Yet that is exactly what Jesus wants to be for us.

Two things make a shepherd *good*. He always leads the sheep where they need to go, and he always gives the sheep what they need to have. And that's why following Jesus is truly the good life. When you are in a difficulty, Jesus will get you where you need to be. When you are desperate, Jesus will give you what you need to have.

In the first century, a shepherd who embarked on a long journey with a flock of sheep was considered successful if he arrived with more than 50 percent of the flock. That world was full of dangers: disease, poisoned grass, bad water, wild animals. But that is why Jesus is a one-of-a-kind shepherd. When Jesus starts out with a hundred sheep, he ends up with a hundred. He doesn't lose any.

You don't have to live an aimless, helpless life of wandering. Jesus invites you to make him the Good Shepherd in your life and become part of his flock. The good life awaits.

This Week's Prayer: *Lord, I am lost without you. This day, and this week, I need you to guide me and to feed me. Thank you for being the Shepherd who is good.*

This Week's Question: Are you living the good life? Have you decided to follow the Shepherd who is good?

8

A Grave Buster

This week's Scriptures:

- John 11:1-44
- Psalm 25:1-5
- Psalm 37:1-11
- Isaiah 40:27-31
- Romans 8:18-25

One Hour a Day

Everyone spends at least an hour waiting every single day. We will spend five years of our lives doing nothing but waiting. We are put on hold, or sit in a doctor's waiting room, or stare at a red light, or impatiently tap our fingers at a checkout counter.

Most of us find it frustrating, aggravating, and irritating. Ask anybody, "What do you like to do for rest and relaxation?" They'll never tell you, "I just like to wait."

But...what...else...can...we...do...except...wait?

The pain of waiting is amplified in a quick-fix, real-time culture. Between the Internet, the computer, the smartphone, and Twitter, we're always in the know and in the now. We'll drive farther and pay more to prevent waiting.

An old Heinz ketchup commercial featured an eager eater waiting for thick rich ketchup to drip out of the bottle. He waited. And waited. Audiences cringed with him. A funny spoof of the same commercial depicted someone, frustrated, tired of waiting, shattering a glass ketchup bottle against a wall.

Have you ever felt like doing that with Jesus? You beg him to show up and intervene, but the clock keeps ticking. Though it feels as maddening as immovable ketchup, Jesus took time to assure us that, no matter how long you wait, he is never late.

The "Why" of Waiting

Why does Jesus sometimes wait? And why does Jesus sometimes make us wait on him?

One of the most famous miracles in the Bible, recorded only in John's Gospel, made a man famous who we would never have known otherwise: Lazarus.

In Israel, the little village of Bethany is just across the Kidron Valley from Jerusalem, not far from the Mount of Olives. A family that lived there—a brother and two sisters—had adopted Jesus into their family, meaning Jesus stayed there whenever he passed through.

Lazarus had fallen deathly ill, and when the sisters send for Jesus, they identify their brother as "the one whom you love." Jesus *did* love Lazarus. They were as brothers.

John writes, "So when he heard that Lazarus was ill, he immediately dropped what he was doing, got to Bethany as fast as he could, and healed Lazarus."

Wait, no. That's actually *not* what John says. But that is precisely what we would expect him to say. Instead we read: "So, when he heard that Lazarus was ill, he *stayed two days longer* in the place where he was" (John 11:6).

What Mary and Martha didn't yet know, but were about to learn, was this: No matter how long you wait, Jesus is never late.

God Is Glorified

Two days after Jesus received news, Lazarus was as dead as disco.

By now even the disciples were probably a little bit incensed. They were thinking to themselves, *Jesus, you've got some explaining to do.* But they should have been listening more carefully because when their Rabbi received news, he said something curious:

> "This illness does not lead to death. It is for the glory of God, so that the Son of God may be glorified through it" (John 11:4).

There are five words in there that not only tell us why Jesus waits, they tell us why he does *everything*. He says that Lazarus's sickness "will not end in death" (John 11:4 NIV).

Wait a minute, you may protest, it *did* end in death. No, Lazarus's sickness *led* to death, but it did not *end* in death. It *ended* in the glory of God because Jesus planned to resurrect his adopted brother.

If you are a believer in Jesus Christ, your life is not going to end in death either. It will *lead* to death, but because you have eternal life, it *ends* in the glory of God.

Whatever Jesus is doing in your life, he's doing it not primarily to satisfy you but to glorify God. The glory of God is the trump card in the deck of life—it will always trump our desires, wants, and preferences.

Faith Is Fortified

When Jesus seems to tarry, we often respond the same way that Martha did when he finally arrived: "'Lord, if you had been here, my brother would not have died'" (John 11:21).

How many times have we said that to Jesus? Lord, if you had done *this*, *that* would not have happened? We know Martha was right. If Jesus had been there, Lazarus would not have died. By the time Jesus returned to Judea, Lazarus had been in a tomb for four days. So there's still that nagging question—why the delay?

This might have made more sense to Jesus's first-century audience. There was a Jewish superstition that when you die, your spirit hovers over your body for up to three days before it departs. So resuscitation is possible at that point. Only after the fourth day, when decomposition sets in, did the spirit finally depart and death was judged irreversible.

If Jesus had arrived two days earlier and resurrected Lazarus, a lot of people would have said, "Lazarus never died. We know how this works. This is no miracle."

But at this point, everyone believed Lazarus was gone, baby, gone.

Jesus's desire was to ignite faith within human hearts. He knew that raising an undeniably dead man would fortify the faith of his friends.

A Concern for Human Hearts

The exchange between Jesus and one of Lazarus's grieving sisters continues when Christ says to Martha,

> "I am the resurrection and the life. Whoever believes in me, though he die, yet shall he live, and everyone who lives and believes in me shall never die. Do you believe this?" (John 11:23-26).

Here is another "I am" statement, and one that would startle many first-century listeners. Most Orthodox Jews believed there would be a resurrection at the end of time, but Jesus wasn't talking about tomorrow, he was talking about today. He was talking about now, not then.

That statement is a game changer because Jesus says to all of us, "As long as you live, I am your life. But when you die, I am your resurrection. I will be there for your present, but I will be there for your future too. I am with you as long as you live, and I am with you when you die."

Martha's issue came down to a single haunting question: "Do you believe this?" Jesus's main concern was not Lazarus's vital signs; he would take care of that. His main concern was Martha's floundering faith.

Whatever challenges you face, Jesus's main concern is not making it all "better," but whether you trust him in the middle of it all. No matter how long you wait, Jesus is never late. And when you wait, miracles happen.

This Week's Prayer: *Lord, grant me patience as I wait for you. Fill my heart with the certainty that, despite what I can see, you are always on time.*

This Week's Question: Are you able to trust Jesus in the midst of whatever challenge or grief you're facing?

9

A One-Way Street

This week's Scriptures:

- John 14:1-6
- Matthew 11:25-30
- John 3:16-21
- Acts 4:5-12
- 1 John 5:9-13

Know This Street?

It's the most famous, most photographed street in America. It stretches only one block long, yet tourists travel from all over the world to drive it. You may not recognize the road's name, but you would probably recognize it in a photo.

The steepness of San Francisco's Lombard Street makes it too dangerous for most vehicles to travel in both directions. So, between 1922 and 1923, part of the road was transformed into a switchback with eight hairpin turns. You could drive only downhill and in a zigzag fashion. Lombard is both the most famous road in our country and a one-way street. People love to drive it, and not one person complains that you can travel only one way.

There is another one-way street that might better be described as *infa*mous. It is not steep, but it is straight. Unlike Lombard, it is the most unpopular one-way street in the world because of where it leads and who it is named after. The street is Jesus, and he claimed it is the only one that leads to God.

You *Do* Know the Way

For three years, the handpicked twelve had followed Jesus 24/7. Everywhere Jesus went, they followed. At the end of his earthly ministry,

Jesus told them where he was about to go, but he also told them they couldn't come there yet. The disciples were both confused and frightened. The one nicknamed "Doubting Thomas" asked, "Lord, we do not know where you are going. How can we know the way?" (John 14:5).

Jesus responds with the most outrageous, politically incorrect, in-your-face statement ever spoken by him: "I am the way, and the truth, and the life. No one comes to the Father except through me" (John 14:6).

That one statement raises more blood pressure, angers more people, and causes more controversy than anything Jesus said. It flies in the face of what the majority of people around the world believe. *Only 25 percent of the world's population claims to be Christian, so who is this minority to be telling the majority that they are wrong and they are lost?*

Here is the good news: It is not *me*. It is not *you*. It is not *we*. The One making that bold, audacious, dogmatic, exclusive, uncompromising, unbending, and unapologetic statement is Jesus. He paints the target on his own back.

Religion Is Not the Way to God

One of the two predominate worldviews that dominate twenty-first-century thinking about God and how to get to him is that *religion* can get you to God. Not a particular religion either—*any* will do.

So how do you explain that Jesus even bothered to come to earth or die on the cross to begin with? If any religion works as well as the next, Good Friday becomes *Dumb* Friday. Why would a loving God allow his Son to experience a brutal execution if it wasn't necessary? We know that religion is not the way to God precisely because Jesus died for the sins of the world and was raised from the dead.

A pastor took a man who loved boxing—and was not at all religious—to a heavyweight fight. Before the match, one of the boxers knelt down in the ring and made the sign of the cross. The man looked at the pastor and asked, "Preacher, what does that mean?" The pastor replied, "It doesn't mean a thing if he can't box!" It doesn't matter how religious you are if you are not on a one-way street called "Jesus."

Righteousness Is Not the Way to God

The second predominate worldview today is that *righteousness* will get you to God. You'll attain it by being a good person and doing the best that you can.

Over the years I've asked thousands of people, "If you were to stand before God and he were to ask, 'Why should I let you into heaven?' what would you say?" Perhaps this is a dated way of phrasing the question, but the responses I've received reveal something universal:

- "I've always tried to be a good person."
- "I've never [insert abominable sin here]."
- "I try to live a good life."

As I reflect on those answers, I realize many people think getting to God is like going to Home Depot. Almost everyone who is in Home Depot has a project they're trying to do on their own. They want to demolish it themselves, repair it themselves, and build it themselves.

They think you have to build your own highway to God. *I can do this myself. I can be good enough. I can be nice enough. I can donate enough. I can work hard enough.* So the orange cones come out and construction begins.

But Jesus tells us that the highway to God is a *freeway*. No toll is required to get on it, and this freeway has already been built and paid for. Anybody can enter anytime they wish.

Only a Relationship Will Get Us to God

Jesus claimed, "No one comes to the Father except through me" (John 14:6). If Jesus is telling the truth, not all roads lead to God. And if Jesus was who he claimed to be and did what he said he did, his claim has to be true.

Between the human race and God stands a barrier called sin. If we are going to be reconciled with a perfect God, that barrier has to be dealt with. We cannot go around it or over it. Sin demands a payment. Jesus came specifically to make that payment. He lived a perfect life and died a sacrificial death to pay for everything we've ever done wrong in the past, present, and future.

If your home is on fire, you had better call a firefighter and not a policeman. If you break a leg, you had better call a doctor and not a firefighter. If your home is broken into, you had better call a policeman and not a doctor. If you are drowning, you had better call a lifeguard, not a plumber. If, as a sinful human being, you want to come to a righteous God, you had better get in touch with the Savior, because he is the only One who can help.

This sets Jesus apart from every other spiritual figure who ever lived. He didn't just say, "Come to me, and I'll show you the way." Jesus said, "I *am* the way."

This Week's Prayer: *Lord, I believe that you are* the *way. Give me courage and boldness to invite others to find life in you alone.*

This Week's Question: If you lived as if Jesus was the *only* way, what would change in your life?

10

The Root of the Fruit

This week's Scriptures:

- John 15:1-11,16
- 1 John 2:1-6
- Galatians 5:16-26

- Isaiah 27:6
- Matthew 13:1-9

Left Behind

When my two older sons were toddlers, my parents would visit us two or three times a year. I loved gathering three generations in one place for playtimes and mealtimes. But one visit is burned into my mind forever.

Whenever Mom and Dad were visiting, my oldest son, James, slept with my mom and my middle son, Jonathan, slept with my dad. Late at night, I could hear my parents tell them stories as they drifted off to dreamland. Some of the most precious pictures I possess were taken of my kids sleeping with their grandparents.

When the final day arrived, Mom and Dad snuck out early in the morning so as not to cause a scene. But on this trip, Jonathan awoke and noticed my dad wasn't in the bed. He ran to the garage just as they were about to pull away and screamed at the top of his lungs, "Don't leave me, Papa! Please don't leave me, Papa!"

A look of grief covered my father's face as their car disappeared over the horizon. When my parents arrived home, my dad called and said, "Son, you just need to be prepared for something. I will never let that happen again. The next time, I am taking those boys back home with me."

Our heavenly Father loves us far more than my mom and dad loved my kids. So, why does he leave us here if he wants to be with us so badly? Or to state it more generally, "What is our purpose for being on earth?"

The answer turns out to be as simple as gardening.

Fruit Bearers

Jesus compares himself to vegetation:

> "I am the true vine, and my Father is the gardener. He cuts off every branch in me that bears no fruit, while every branch that does bear fruit he prunes so that it will be even more fruitful" (John 15:1-2 NIV).

Most likely, Jesus had just left the place where he'd eaten the Last Supper with his disciples. He was walking to the Garden of Gethsemane, a landscape full of vines. When properly cultivated, these vines produced grapes used to make wine.

In Jesus's teaching, God is the gardener, Jesus is the vine, and we are the branches. The gardener's only concern is the branch. He wants the branch to bear the fruit that the vine produces, which means the fruit here is the character of Christ.

For what purpose has God put people on this planet? Jesus says, *to bear fruit.*

One sure sign that you are following Jesus is that your life is bearing fruit that others can see, taste, and touch. When you are connected to the root of Christ, you will bear the fruit of Christ.

Jesus Wants to Connect with You Personally

Jesus's image of the vine illustrates the intimate connection he wants with his followers. This teaching sets Christianity apart from other religions. No other faith offers its followers a personal union with its founder. The Buddhist does not claim to be joined with Buddha. The Confucianist does not claim to be joined to Confucius. The Muslim does not claim to be joined to Mohammed, but Christians claim to be connected to, joined to Jesus.

This is a point of confusion for many outside the Christian faith.

They confuse religion with relationship. They think Christians are following a dead man rather than connecting to a living God. Following Jesus is not just an *organizational* connection with a church, but an *organic* connection with Christ. Some have done the former rather than the latter, and then they wonder why their faith is fallow and lifeless.

We were created to be organically joined to Christ's life just as branches are connected to a vine.

Jesus Wants You to Concentrate on Him Perpetually

When Jesus teaches that God is a gardener, he reminds us that God cares for us and wants us to be fruitful. When Jesus calls himself the vine, he tells us what the fruit should look like. Fruit always reflects the character of its source. An apple tree always produces apples. A pear tree always produces pears. You won't plant a grapevine that produces tomatoes. In the same way, Jesus-followers should produce the character of the Christ they are connected to.

Of course, the gardener's first concern for the branch is not just that it bears fruit, but that it bears *much* fruit. Jesus talks about a progression in this matter of fruit bearing.

According to Jesus, some branches bear no fruit. Some branches bear some fruit. Others bear more fruit. And then some branches bear *much* fruit. Jesus is saying, "Connect yourself to me, and I'll produce an abundance of fruit in your life."

Finally he talks about a branch that bears the best fruit.

> "You did not choose me, but I chose you and appointed you that you should go and bear fruit and that your fruit should abide, so that whatever you ask the Father in my name, he may give it to you" (John 15:16).

This is the fruit that lasts! This is fruit that won't rot. It just continues to ripen.

If you want to bear the fruit of Christ, you have to connect with and concentrate on Christ.

A Diligent Pruner

Sometimes branches have sucker-shoots, which are tiny outgrowths emerging from where the vine and the branch intersect. They suck the sap from the vine that ought to be going to the branch. If sucker-shoots are not pruned, the branch becomes malnourished.

God often uses the shears of circumstance, tough times, heartache, difficulty, the loss of a job, or a physical ailment to prune us. Though we don't realize it, he is trimming from our lives those sucker-shoots that are leaching the sap out of the vine and preventing us from bearing fruit.

Other times, God uses the scissors of Scripture. Jesus announces, "Already you are clean because of the word that I have spoken to you" (John 15:3). The word for "clean" is the same word for "prune." Often you read your Bible, and you get convicted and don't know why. God is cutting away the bad so it doesn't get in the way of the good.

Pruning is painful. Pruning hurts. Pruning cuts.

Yet the gardener prunes because he considers the branch important and wants to maximize its fruitfulness. The hand of the gardener is never closer to the branch than when he is pruning.

This Week's Prayer: *Lord, help me to recognize you as the Master Gardener who is the caretaker of my soul.*

This Week's Question: How has God lovingly pruned you during difficult seasons of your life to make you more like Jesus?

SECTION THREE

Jesus, the Miracle Worker

Jesus was the greatest wonder-worker who ever lived. He calmed a sea after a storm whipped it into a frenzy. He walked on water, and transformed it into wine. Jesus fed thousands with the equivalent of a Happy Meal and never met a disease he couldn't heal. But these miracles are more than magic tricks. They reveal surprising truths about who Jesus is and spiritual lessons about how we can know and relate to him.

11

A Man of Marvels

This week's Scriptures:

- Matthew 15:29-31
- Mark 2:8-12
- John 14:8-14
- Matthew 7:21-23
- John 10:22-39

Do You Believe?

With 2.5 seconds left on the clock, Olympic hockey commentator Al Michaels screams, "Do you believe in miracles?"

The unbelievable upset—the United States hockey team beat Russia and went on to win the gold medal in the 1980 Winter Olympics—was as close to a miracle in the sports world as you may ever see. But, of course, a miracle did not actually occur.

Here's my working definition for "miracles": *Acts of God that use or exceed the laws of nature to perform humanly impossible feats to reveal God's power and glorify him.*

A miracle assumes God *can* perform miracles and also that God *does*.

The Smithsonian Institute in Washington displays a leather-bound book called the Jefferson Bible. This bound volume was the third president's own version of the Bible that he read every day until he died. Using a razor, Jefferson had cut and pasted selected verses from the four Gospels, in chronological order, and removed every reference to a miracle found in any of them. This is a Gospel that excludes the two central miracles of Christianity: the incarnation and the resurrection. So Jefferson rejected both the God who performs miracles and the miracles performed by God.

But Jesus Christ is defined by the miraculous—from his virgin birth to his sinless life to his resurrection. Two of the four Gospels commence with a miracle that C.S. Lewis called the "Grand Miracle": the incarnation of Jesus Christ, God becoming man. If you believe in the incarnation, then you have no trouble believing in miracles. And if you believe in miracles, you're one step closer to fully knowing the One who changed everything.

Opening Our Minds to Miracles

The Bible *begins* with a miracle: God speaking a world into existence. Regardless of how you interpret the Genesis story, something was created out of nothing. That is a miracle!

Often people comment, "The Bible is not a science textbook. Miracles have nothing to do with science. Therefore, it is irrelevant what the Bible says since it deals only with history and theology." But you can't fully separate science, history, or theology.

Take for example the central miracle of the Christian faith, which is the resurrection of Jesus Christ. Is his resurrection a theological truth, a historical truth, or a scientific truth? The answer to that question is yes. Scientifically, a resurrected body deals with anatomy, biology, physics, and chemistry. Historically, there's probably more proof that it happened than for any other miracle in the history of the world. Theologically, it is the foundation of the Christian faith.

If you accept the Bible as a historically reliable book, not to mention the Word of God, then it doesn't matter what other people believe. The evidence for miracles, particularly in the life of Jesus, is overwhelming.

Jesus's Miracles Authenticated His Mission

The first purpose of miracles is *authentication*. Jesus performed miracles to authenticate what he said and who he was. One of the most popular terms used for miracles in the Gospels is the word *sign*. A sign points to or indicates something else. The miracles of Jesus were signs pointing to the fact that he was God and that what he said was true.

There is a story in the Gospels about four men who let a paralytic down through the roof of a house so that Jesus would heal him. When they brought the man to Jesus, the first thing Jesus said was, "Son, your sins are forgiven." The scribes who were there went berserk, thinking to themselves: *Why does this man speak like that? He is blaspheming! Who can forgive sins but God alone?* Jesus, knowing what they were thinking, replied, "Which is easier, to say to the paralytic, 'Your sins are forgiven,' or to say, 'Rise, take up your bed and walk'?" (Mark 2:5-9).

Everyone listening knew the answer to Jesus's question. Obviously it is easier to claim to forgive sins. No one can prove whether that happened or not. But then Jesus healed the paralyzed man and for the first time he walked home. The miracle authenticated that Jesus was on a messianic mission to forgive sinners.

Jesus's Miracles Reveal Who He Is

The second purpose of miracles is *revelation*. Jesus's divine claims incensed the religious leaders and eventually got him crucified. As John explains, it almost got him killed *before* the cross (John 10:22-39). The Jews were prepared to stone him to death after he said, "I and the Father are one" (v. 30). To any Jew, this was blasphemy.

Jesus protests, though, by insisting that he was only doing his Father's work. He basically says, "Look, if you don't want to believe what I say, fine. But at least believe what I do. If you don't want to believe my *words*, at least believe my *works*."

I read a true story about Paul Doré, a brilliant nineteenth-century French artist, who lost his passport in a foreign country. When he arrived at the border, he explained his problem to the immigration official and told him who he was. The official handed Doré paper and a pencil and said, "Draw a picture of Paris with the Eiffel Tower in the background." Within a few minutes, Doré produced an exact replica of the city and convinced the official he was who he claimed to be just by what he drew.

That is exactly what the miracles of Jesus were for—to reveal he was who he claimed to be: God's only Son.

Jesus's Miracles Glorify the Father

The third purpose of miracles is *glorification*. After Jesus healed that paralytic, in body and in spirit, Matthew attests, "When the crowds saw it…they glorified God, who had given such authority to men" (Matthew 9:8).

The ultimate purpose of everything that Jesus said and did was to glorify his Father. Whether or not a miracle gives glory to God will actually help you to discern the difference between miracles and black magic, between true and false displays of supernatural power. Jesus gave this warning:

> "On that day many will say to me, 'Lord, Lord, did we not prophesy in your name, and cast out demons in your name, and do many mighty works in your name?' And then will I declare to them, 'I never knew you; depart from me, you workers of lawlessness'" (Matthew 7:22-23).

Jesus offers two warnings about miracles. He said that a miracle is not necessarily always from God, even when performed by someone who calls Jesus "Lord." *The message always trumps the miracle.* If someone performs a miracle, but at the same time they are teaching unbiblical things, forget the miracle and the miracle worker.

Second, a miracle is not necessarily from God just because it helps people. Some actually cast out demons apart from the power of Christ. They did a good work and their miracles helped the afflicted, but they didn't derive from God.

The first two purposes for why Jesus performed miracles—authentication and revelation—are no longer necessary. We have God's Word for this. Yet God often still works miracles for glorification, which is why we should expect Jesus to work wonders in our lives. Because God—because Jesus—always has been and always will be in the glorifying business.

As Al Michaels once asked, "Do you believe in miracles?" If so, expect that Jesus still can and wants to perform them in your life.

This Week's Prayer: *Lord, because of the miracles you've worked in the past, I believe you are who you say you are. Glorify yourself today through me.*

This Week's Question: Do you believe in miracles?

12

Crisis Manager

This week's Scriptures:

- John 2:1-11
- 1 Peter 5:6-11
- John 13:12-20

- Matthew 11:25-30
- Matthew 6:25-34

Spectacular (and Unspectacular) Debuts

On April 23, 1952, Hoyt Wilhelm—the greatest knuckleball pitcher to ever play baseball—came to the plate for the first time in his major-league career. On the first pitch he ever swung at, he hit a home run over the right-field fence. Why was that so unusual? Although he played twenty-one seasons, Hoyt Wilhelm never hit another one.

You could not script that kind of debut any better.

But the most interesting and puzzling debut I've ever encountered was Jesus's as he begins his public ministry.

Let's say your public relations firm has been given the job of planning Jesus's entry into earthly ministry. You gather around the boardroom table and decide that the best way to do it is for Jesus to perform a miracle. Ideas start flying.

"Let's have him raise someone from the dead," someone says. "No. Let's have him feed thousands of people with a Happy Meal," another suggests. "What about having him walk on water?" a third says. Everyone agrees it should be spectacular.

But Jesus's first miracle is probably the simplest, most unspectacular that he ever performed. Jesus and his disciples are at a wedding when the host runs out of wine. All the stores are closed, and Jesus's mother asks for help. So Jesus transforms six large jars of water into wine (John 2:1-11). That's it. That's his debut. That is his first swing at the plate.

A Big Deal Miracle

This miracle *was* a big deal, though, because it points to something significant.

The hosts and guests that day were running on empty. There will be times in your life—you may be there now—when you are running on empty too. You've got a problem that you can't solve. You are in a crisis you can't handle. You are in a hole you can't dig yourself out of. You are at the end of your rope. You are running on empty. *But our problems are Jesus's possibilities.*

This simple miracle teaches us a profound lesson on what to do when we are empty:

- Turn to Jesus when you face problems.
- Talk to Jesus about your problems.
- Trust Jesus to handle your problems.

The next time an unexpected crisis pops up (and it will), the next time life goes south when you are driving north, remember a wedding, a woman, water, and wine, and you just might experience something supernatural in your life.

Turn to Jesus When You Face Problems

The host's problem was that the wine was gone. At that time, wine at a wedding was like cake today. Can you imagine attending a wedding where they forgot the cake?

Like this one, the majority of problems that we face every day are not life-and-death problems. Losing your job or losing your car keys are not the same thing as losing your life, though they are real problems. Facing a lawsuit or even jail is not like facing death, though it is still a real problem. The problems you face are not as important as how you face your problems.

Mary responds the way we ought to whenever we face a troubling situation: she turns to Jesus. She doesn't push the panic button. Mary's blood pressure doesn't rise, and she doesn't tear her hair out. Instead, she turns to Jesus and tells him about the problem.

Jesus wants to hear about what vexes and plagues us. You may think, *But he already knows what my problems are.* That's true, but Jesus wants you to tell him what those problems are just the same.

Talk to Jesus About Your Problems

There was not a bigger social happening in Jewish life than a wedding. It usually began with a ceremony at sundown in the synagogue. Then the entire wedding party would leave the synagogue and begin this long candlelight procession through the middle of town. The couple would be escorted past as many homes as possible so everyone could come out and congratulate them. After the procession, the couple didn't go on a honeymoon; the honeymoon was brought to them. They went home to a party lasting several days!

There would be gift-giving, speech-making, wining and dining. Hospitality at a wedding was considered such a sacred duty that the master at the wedding could actually be sued for "breach of hospitality." So running out of food or wine was considered a tremendous insult.

Mary makes the 9-1-1 call to Jesus because she knew that *what matters to us matters to Jesus.*

We believe Jesus cares about big stuff like cancer, bankruptcy, divorce, or death. But Jesus also cares about grouchy bosses, flat tires, lost dogs, broken dishes, late flights, toothaches, and ruptured disks.

The Bible says, "Give *all* your worries and cares to God, for he cares about you" (1 Peter 5:7 NLT, emphasis added).

What matters to us matters to Jesus.

Trust Jesus to Handle Your Problems

Mary instructs the servants, "Do whatever he tells you" (John 2:5).

What a great piece of advice! Jesus never met a problem that he could not solve if the afflicted only do what he tells them to. Too many of us know what Jesus wants us to do, but refuse to do it. Jesus said, "If you know these things, blessed are you if you do them" (John 13:17).

We often assume that obedience follows blessing. And sometimes it does. When God gives to us, we should respond with devotion out of joy. But in this story, the water was not transformed until the jars were filled to the brim the way Jesus requested. Often, blessing follows obedience.

Jesus tells the servants to draw out some of the water and take it to the master of ceremonies to taste. Those jars normally held water that was used to wash dirty hands, not wine for a wedding. These men could have been sent to prison for such a disgraceful act. But they obeyed anyway.

Their obedience *to* Jesus led to great blessing *from* Jesus. So it is with our lives.

This Week's Prayer: *Lord, I thank you that I can trust you with any problem in my life, knowing that you will handle it. Teach me to let go.*

This Week's Question: What problem do you need to release into Jesus's care?

13

Captain of My Ship

This week's Scriptures:

- Mark 4:35-40
- Psalm 107:23-32
- Proverbs 3:5-6
- Psalm 31:1-24
- John 14:25-27

Rough Waters

Each time my wife and I visit the Holy Land, we take a boat ride across the Sea of Galilee to Capernaum. This ancient city contains the ruins of a synagogue where Jesus actually taught. And yet the trip that has always been so peaceful once gave me a jolt I'll never forget.

Mountains filled with deep ravines surround the Sea of Galilee. Those ravines serve as huge funnels bringing cold air from the mountains into a collision with hot air above the water. The clash, as I learned the hard way, can produce a storm in a flash.

We were halfway across the sea on one trip when the sky grew black and the wind whipped. Rain began to fall—one drop and then one thousand. The boat began to swing high and then slap the waves. In that moment, I could understand how the disciples must have felt when the same occurrence happened to them.

By the time we arrived on the other side, I wanted to kiss the beach. After the trepidation faded, I realized that my experience is the way life works out sometimes.

- You come home from work, walk into the kitchen, and find a note saying, "I want out of the marriage." A clap of thunder!

- You go to the doctor anticipating a normal checkup, and the lab work comes back and you have cancer. The wind howls!

- You go to bed at peace, only to be interrupted by a phone call at three in the morning telling you that your father has suddenly died of a heart attack. Your ship nearly capsizes!

The only predictable thing about life's storms is their unpredictability. They sweep in when you least expect them. Jesus knew this, so he performed a miracle once to teach us how to weather the storms.

Jesus Wants Us to Remember His Promises

On the banks of the Sea of Galilee, Jesus invited his disciples, "Let us go across to the other side" (Mark 4:35).

The disciples should have known that when Jesus climbed into the boat, it became unsinkable. Because implicit in Jesus's words is a promise that they would arrive safely.

Like the disciples, however, there is a difference between hearing a promise and believing it. We too fail to believe that Jesus will do what he has promised us. In those moments, we should remind ourselves that the sun may quit shining, the wind may start blowing, and the waves may begin crashing, but Jesus never fails to keep his promises.

When Tiger Woods was five years old, he asked his father to buy him a tricycle. Earl Woods told his son he would have to think about it. Every day Tiger would ask for the tricycle, and Earl would respond that he was still thinking about it. After a few months, Earl finally said to Tiger, "Okay. I promise you I will get that tricycle."

He was stunned by Tiger's reaction. Tiger didn't jump up and down with joy. He didn't ask his dad to immediately go buy it. The older Woods said, "I got absolutely no reaction at all." Then it dawned on him: "Tiger believed me when I made a promise."

This is how Jesus wants us to respond to him. With trust and obedience. The moment that Jesus made that promise, the disciples could have all gone to sleep. They could have all sat on that deck, soaked up the sun, and read a good book on their Kindle. Because they had the promise of Jesus, and you can always count on him.

Jesus Wants Us to Rest in His Presence

As the disciples are sailing, a choppy windstorm blows in. This wasn't a spring shower, a cloudburst, or even a hard downpour. In Matthew's account of this event, the Greek word he uses to describe the storm is *seismos*, a word used elsewhere in the New Testament to describe violent earthquakes, such as the ones that occurred at Jesus's death and again at his resurrection. This was the kind of tempest that could shatter their ship into toothpicks.

When storms come, we might assume they are a result of something we've done wrong or that we are outside of God's will. *Maybe I disobeyed God and made him angry*, we think.

But the disciples were not in the storm due to disobedience, but rather because of *obedience*. They had not done something wrong, but something right. They hadn't made a misstep; rather, they walked exactly where Jesus asked them to.

Even if you live as holy a life as is possible and fall deeply in love with Jesus, you will still face storms. Many times these squalls come when we are closest to Jesus, as the disciples were about to learn.

Jesus Wants Us to Rely on His Power

Jesus awoke because the disciples were in full meltdown mode, begging him to save their lives. So Jesus crawled off the cushion he was sleeping on, stepped into the chaos, and said to the sea, "Peace! Be still!" (Mark 4:39). And in a blink, the water was smoother than silk.

Jesus's words here—"Peace! Be still!"—literally mean "to muzzle or silence." He has told the tempest, "Sit down and shut up!" Like slapping a muzzle on a barking dog, quiet emerged.

In this story, Jesus does not keep the storm from striking the boat, but he did keep the storm from *sinking* the boat. When Jesus told those disciples they were going to cross over, he didn't promise smooth sailing. He just guaranteed a safe landing.

You must face the difficulties of your life either with fear or faith. What is the difference? Fear focuses on the storm. Faith focuses on the Savior.

It may sound shocking, but *we need storms*. Christ allows us to sail into them so we'll remember his promises, rest in his presence, and rely on his power.

I don't know what storm you are going through right now, what storm you are coming out of, or what storm you may be heading into. But Jesus wants you to turn your face toward him and remember that there is no need to fear when he is near. That's why he wants to be the Captain of your life's ship.

The Safe Place

The stern on a fishing boat was the only place to hide from the weather and the only place with enough space and protection to drift off to sleep. It was enclosed and the only protected part of the boat.

Jesus had crawled into the stern, and Mark notes that he had even taken a cushion. Why does Mark add that particular detail? Because Jesus didn't just nod off by accident. This was a premeditated nap!

When the storm arrives, Jesus was at peace while the other disciples were going to pieces. He remembered what they had forgotten: they were right where God wanted them to be. Just as he was with the disciples, so God was with him.

In every storm you go through, you always have the presence, power, and promises of Christ. You may not always be aware of Jesus, but he is there just the same. For those disciples, the safest place in the world at that exact moment was right there in that boat. Because safety is not the absence of problems. Safety is the presence of Jesus.

Whenever you stare down a storm, remember there is no need to fear when Jesus is near!

This Week's Prayer: *Lord, I believe there is no need to fear when you are near. Be near to me this day.*

This Week's Question: What does it look like to trust Jesus during the storm you're facing?

14

A Miraculous Multiplier

This week's Scriptures:

- John 6:1-14
- Proverbs 11:24
- Luke 6:37-38
- Malachi 3:6-12
- Matthew 25:14-30

The Law of Leftovers

Thanksgiving dinner is my favorite meal of the year. It's not just what I get to eat that makes it special, but also who I get to eat it with. All of my favorite dishes are right in front of me: the turkey I cooked along with the homemade dressing, my wife's out-of-this-world sweet potato soufflé, my sister in-law's macaroni-n-cheese, yeast rolls, green bean casserole, and honey ham. As I walk up to the table, my family gathers with me and the world seems all right.

Every Thanksgiving brings with it the twin promises of food and leftovers. The latter is a sign that everybody got all they wanted, nobody went away hungry, and there is still enough to do it all over again. This holiday meal illustrates a principle I call "The Law of the Leftovers."

I have more food at Thanksgiving than I have at any other time of the year, and I feed more people. Yet even with twenty-five to thirty people in our home, we always have leftovers!

The Law of Leftovers is expressed in an ancient Scripture passage written over twenty-five hundred years ago by the wisest man who ever lived. Solomon stated the law this way:

One gives freely, yet grows all the richer;
another withholds what he should give,
and only suffers want.

(Proverbs 11:24)

According to the Law of the Leftovers, when I bless others, I receive the greatest blessing.

Jesus Asks You for What You Have

One of Jesus's most famous miracles—"the feeding of the five thousand"—operates on this principle. This is the only miracle Matthew, Mark, Luke, and John all include. It marks the only recorded time Jesus ever asked somebody's advice about what to do. And this feeding had the largest audience of all Christ's miracles.

Around six in the evening, Jesus and the disciples find themselves stranded with a crowd out in the country. A crisis is brewing as the sun sets: people are hungry. Jesus wonders aloud to Philip about where to buy bread for everyone.

Philip was doubtlessly dumbfounded. The men alone numbered about five thousand, but women and children were also present. When you consider how large ancient families were before the advent of birth control, scholars estimate that crowd may have totaled more than twenty-five thousand.

But Jesus wasn't really asking Philip a question. He was giving the disciple a test. "He said this to test him," John wrote, "for he himself knew what he would do" (John 6:6).

When Jesus asks you for anything, trust that it isn't just a request but a test.

Give What You Have to Jesus

Philip pulls out his calculator and figures that it would take about eight months of an average worker's wages to purchase that much food. He thinks he is off the hook.

There was no place to buy that much food, and even if there were, they didn't have enough money to pay for it or enough time to get it. Philip is thinking, *For the first time in your life, Jesus, I have stumped you!*

Jesus's heart shatters. What bothered Jesus wasn't the lack of food, but the lack of faith. Philip flunks the test.

But just when it appears that all is lost, Andrew presents a boy whose mama had had enough sense to pack him a lunchbox with some loaves of bread and a few fish. The poor boy's meal was more meager than many have imagined it. A loaf was a small, brittle wafer about the size of a mini-pancake. The word for fish refers to sea creatures about the size of sardines.

The little boy had a little lunch. But what made that little lunch a big feast is what he did when Jesus asked for it.

The boy gave it to him.

Jesus Will Use What You Give

When Jesus asks the disciples to have everyone sit down for supper, I imagine a few wanted to call a psychiatrist. But then Jesus does something outrageous. He gives thanks! Why was Jesus grateful for a tiny meal that could barely feed a child in the midst of a hungry crowd.

This is how God operates: Jesus asks for what he desires. We give to Jesus what he asks. Jesus uses what we give. Even the smallest gifts.

God has a habit of using little things to accomplish unbelievable things: a shepherd boy's slingshot, the change in a widow's purse, a poverty-stricken teenage virgin, and seed-sized faith.

Do you know what determines something's value? The one whose hands it's put into. You can buy a professional baseball online for about twelve dollars. If you put it into the hands of a major-league pitcher, it is worth millions. In the same way, what made that little boy's lunch so valuable was not its size but his willingness to offer it to Jesus.

Anything you have is valuable if you are willing to give it to Christ.

Jesus Blesses What He Uses

When they'd finished eating, the leftovers filled twelve baskets. Can you imagine? The original lunch didn't fill up even a single basket, and now the leftovers overflowed a dozen. Jesus always blesses what he uses.

I love this story about Jesus because the little boy in the story is you and me. We all have lunches in our possession. We all have talents, abilities, time, and resources that Jesus would like to use.

The boy didn't say, "Lord, you can have *one* of the fish, but I'll keep the other one. You take *three* of the loaves, and I'll keep the other two." He gave Jesus *everything* Jesus asked for.

If you want to experience the Law of the Leftovers and watch Jesus add to what he subtracts from you and multiply it, you've got to give him everything. When you do, you will find others will be blessed and you will get to enjoy the leftovers.

This Week's Prayer: *Lord, teach me to trust you with my lunch, confident that you will provide abundantly and bless others through my offering.*

This Week's Question: Have you given generously to God, or are you holding back?

15

A Leader Worth Following

> **This week's Scriptures:**
>
> - Luke 7:1-10
> - Romans 13:1-7
> - Ephesians 5:22–6:9
> - Hebrews 13:17
> - John 6:35-40

The Leader Who Follows

Only twice does the Bible say that Jesus was "amazed" at something. And both were, to one degree or another, related to leadership.

Do you consider yourself a leader?

All of us are in some capacity. Mothers lead children. Husbands lead families. Managers lead employees. CEOs and COOs and CFOs and presidents and vice presidents lead managers. If you are an older child, you lead your younger siblings. If you're a student, some of your peers look up to you whether you realize it or not.

Mark writes that Jesus was "amazed" that people in his hometown did not believe in him (Mark 6:1-6 NIV). They did not want to let Jesus lead them or influence their lives with his good news. Jesus was wonder struck that people he had grown up with, who had known him all his life and had watched him firsthand, did not believe in him. They didn't believe and they wouldn't be led by him.

Luke tells us that Jesus was also "amazed" by a man who *did* believe in him (Luke 7:1-10 NIV).

The man was a centurion, an officer in the Roman guard. He wasn't particularly religious. He was no Bible scholar. What amazed Jesus about this man was not just *that* he believed in him, but *how* he believed. The centurion understood a key principle of Jesus's leadership philosophy: the way to lead is to learn how to follow.

Under Authority

This centurion had a sick servant. The man had heard about Jesus, so he sent some Jewish elders to ask Jesus to heal the servant. Jesus chose to go with them, and when he was not far from the house, the centurion sent some friends to say to him, "You don't need to come any farther. I understand leadership, and I understand authority. You have both the leadership and the authority to just speak the word and my servant will be healed." He believed that Jesus could have spoken the order without moving a muscle, and the servant would have been healed.

To prove that he understood Jesus's leadership paradigm, he continued, "For I too am a man set under authority, with soldiers under me: and I say to one, 'Go,' and he goes; and to another, 'Come,' and he comes; and to my servant, 'Do this,' and he does it" (Luke 7:8). He said, "Look, I know what it is to tell a person to 'come' and he comes and to tell a person to 'go' and he goes. I understand leadership."

Pecking Order

Have you ever thought about where the term *pecking order* comes from? Norwegian scientists came up with it while studying the barnyard social system. By counting the number of times chickens give and receive pecks, these scientists discerned a chain of command. The "alpha" bird does most of the pecking and the "omega" bird gets pecked the most. The rest of the chickens fall somewhere in between.

But God has built a pecking order into all of life.

There is a pecking order between a government and its citizens. Romans 13:1 says, "Let every person be subject to the governing authorities. For there is no authority except from God, and those that exist have been instituted by God." There is a pecking order in the home. Ephesians 5 says the husband is to lead the wife and in Ephesians 6 we're told that parents are to lead their children.

From the time we were born, the first lesson Jesus wanted us to learn was not how to lead but how to follow. The first lesson Jesus wants you to learn is not how to be over but how to be under.

Respecting Leadership

No one can deny that America has experienced cultural and moral breakdown in the last thirty years. One of the key drivers is a loss of respect for leadership.

The first lesson Jesus taught his disciples was, "Follow me, and I will make you fishers of men" (Mark 1:7). Jesus was saying, "If you will let me teach you how to follow, I will help you learn how to lead." It is not coincidental that most of his disciples went on to become the first leaders of the early church. For three years, they learned how to follow.

If you do not learn how to respect others' leadership, then others will refuse to respect yours.

This is why fathers must learn to follow Christ. Many kids don't follow the leadership of their fathers because their father does not follow Christ's leadership. You will never know how to lead if you don't learn how to follow.

Many mothers can't control their children because they have refused to follow the leadership of their husbands.

A lot of teenagers are depressed, have trouble in their relationships, and are frustrated because they refuse to respect their parents' leadership. The same with students with their teachers and employees with their bosses.

When you learn how to recognize and respect leadership, when you know how to follow, you'll learn how to lead.

Receiving Leadership

When Jesus heard the centurion's faith and understanding, Jesus *marveled* at him and healed his servant.

Amazing! Jesus could perform miracles for a Gentile stranger that he could not do for his Jewish friends and family, all because the centurion understood how to receive Jesus's leadership.

Even Jesus followed the principle of leading by following first.

- Jesus followed his parents. Luke notes, "[Jesus] was submissive to [his parents]" (Luke 2:51).
- Jesus followed his Father. In John 6:38, he said this about his relationship to his Father, "For I have come down from heaven, not to do my own will but the will of him who sent me."
- Jesus followed the Spirit. Luke announces that Jesus "was led by the Spirit in the wilderness" (Luke 4:1).

Somehow we have gotten the idea that being under leadership binds us, restrains us, and restricts us. Following leadership is not a chain that binds you; it is a key that frees you.

The church today would be revolutionized if its people were eager to learn how to follow. It would be revolutionized if its people were willing to serve when called on by its leaders or if they would give gladly and generously when leaders called for help.

Leading, in any sphere of your life, is about learning how to follow the leadership and the lordship of Jesus Christ, because he is the ultimate leader.

This Week's Prayer: *Lord, teach me—in the sphere of my everyday living—what it means to be a faithful follower of you.*

This Week's Question: Have you learned from your life experience how to follow?

16

The Great Empathizer

This week's Scriptures:

- Mark 2:1-12
- Mark 9:14-29
- Romans 3:9-20
- Romans 5:1-11
- Hebrews 4:14-16

Divine Excitement

Few things really excite me. I get excited when I get to spend time with my sons or go on a romantic getaway with my wife. I get excited when my grandson and granddaughter remind me they love their "Pop." I get excited when my Georgia Bulldogs football team wins (and anytime our rivals lose). Warm, homemade chocolate-chip cookies make the list.

What excites Jesus?

He gives us some clues in his encounter with a paraplegic man. Whether because of a fall or because he was born this way, this man was physically disabled. The Greek word means "to be loosed on one side." If he was going to get to Jesus, somebody needed to bring him.

The day his best chance arrived, a crowd gathered to hear Jesus teach from inside a house. Now the challenge was intensified. Even if this man could have gotten *up*, he couldn't have gotten *in*. The house was full. People jammed the doorways. Kids sat in the windows. Nobody could move. All the seats were occupied, and this man was not able to stand.

Our story begins here because in the midst of this scene Jesus gets excited. Why?

Jesus gets excited when he sees our faith.

Faith to Approach Jesus

This man had four buddies who heard that the healing rabbi was in town, and they were determined to get their friend a meeting with the man.

> They couldn't bring him to Jesus because of the crowd, so they dug a hole through the roof above his head. Then they lowered the man on his mat, right down in front of Jesus (Mark 2:4 NLT).

You've got to admire these guys' determination. Even though they couldn't go in, their faith wouldn't let them give up. In the first century, many roofs were made of dried palm branches combined with clay and laid across beams, somewhat like tile. Tearing a hole in this kind of material was fairly easy. The men scaled the outside of the house and installed a skylight.

They could have fallen and injured themselves. They could have dropped their friend to the floor. Worse, they were going to interrupt Jesus right in the middle of his sermon. But none of this seemed to matter. They saw their chance and, by faith, took it, believing that Jesus would heal their friend.

Only one reason would have motivated these men to go to all that trouble: they believed Christ could and would heal their friend. But instead of offering healing, Jesus says something strange.

> Seeing their faith, Jesus said to the paralyzed man, "My child, your sins are forgiven" (Mark 2:5 NLT).

The man's friends are confused. The man was probably a bit disappointed. The owner of the house was ticked off that his roof was damaged. And the religious hypocrites in the crowd weren't happy that someone claimed to forgive sins. But Jesus was grinning like a Cheshire cat, because he saw real faith.

An Unlikely Remedy

Think about those four friends up on the roof. They are hot, dirty, sweaty, and probably facing a lawsuit. The crowd thinks they are a bunch of nuts. They carried their friend to a healer, and instead they got a preacher. Or if you asked the Pharisees, a blasphemer.

And what about the paraplegic? He is lying there thinking, *Great, I can't walk, and you want to preach to me? What is wrong with this picture?*

But Jesus knew that the man's greatest problem wasn't sickness but sin. While sickness was his most *pressing* problem, sin was his *primary* problem. While the man assumed the greatest gift Jesus could give him was to *heal* him, Jesus knew a better present was to *save* him.

If you want to know why cancer cells show up in the body, babies die, drunk drivers kill innocents, childbirth causes pain, or tragedies fall on selfless monks, you have to go all the way back to the first three chapters of Genesis. Sorrow, suffering, and death are all ultimately caused by sin.

That matters because if sin is our greatest problem, then forgiveness is our greatest need.

God Shows His Faithfulness

This man was disabled, but he was primarily disabled by sin. Jesus loved him too much to deal with his symptom and not his problem. Every problem, every struggle, every illness, every heartache, every pain you have is a physical reminder that your greatest need is spiritual. Most of this world doesn't understand that and neither did the crowd surrounding Jesus that day.

> And the man did it—got up, grabbed his stretcher, and walked out, with everyone there watching him. They rubbed their eyes, incredulous—and then praised God, saying, "We've never seen anything like this!" (Mark 2:12 MSG).

They were so excited about the physical, but Jesus was excited about the spiritual. They were so excited about the temporary; Jesus was so excited about the eternal. They were so excited this man could now walk. Jesus was so excited because this man could now worship.

Why I Am a Christian

That is why I am a Christian.

Christianity is the only spiritual philosophy that addresses our greatest problem, which is sin, and meets our greatest need, which is forgiveness. If my sins have been forgiven, if my place is secured in heaven, if I no longer have to fear death, then I can face anything else. When I can stand before a holy and righteous God and declare that because of the cross my sins are forgiven, Jesus gets excited.

This Week's Prayer: *Lord, I believe that you can use me to bring people to you. Use me, this week, to meet people's deepest needs.*

This Week's Question: Day to day, are you more keenly aware of your pressing need or your primary need?

17

The Divine Ophthalmologist

This week's Scriptures:

- John 9:1-41
- Matthew 4:12-16
- John 1:1-18
- John 3:16-21
- Acts 26:12-18

Spiritual Blindness

Augustine, one of the early church fathers, was once approached by a pagan who showed him his idol and said, "Here is my god. Where is yours?" Augustine replied, "I cannot show you my God—not because there is no God to show you, but because you have no eyes to see him."

In the Bible, we read about a man who was blind from the moment human hands pulled him from his mother's womb. In the first century, if you had a debilitating condition—blindness, deafness, leprosy, paralysis, or some other chronic illness—your only hope was for family members to care for you. A person like this was viewed as a burden and a curse.

The man we encounter in John chapter 9 entered into a world where the velvet cover of darkness had been pulled over the light of the sun. He entered the world in desperation. But this man had never met Jesus. (At that time, most of the world didn't know who Jesus was and had never seen him.)

If you don't have Jesus, you are living in spiritual darkness. You could have perfect twenty-twenty vision but spiritually be blind as a bat—because you not only have eyes in your head, you also have eyes in your heart. People who refuse to believe in Jesus Christ don't have a physical problem. They have a spiritual problem.

What Did He Do to Deserve This?

People around the blind man believed—as did most first-century Jews—that his physical disability was due either to *his* sin or *his parents'* sin. In their mind, if you were handicapped, you were not just physically disabled, you were also spiritually and morally tainted. That's why the disciples asked Jesus, "Rabbi, who sinned, this man or his parents, that he was born blind?" (John 9:2).

When people saw someone in this condition, they asked, "I wonder what this person did to deserve this?" They assumed that a physical handicap was a sign of God's displeasure.

Jesus's reply was revolutionary: "It was not that this man sinned, or his parents, but that the works of God might be displayed in him" (John 9:3).

- The man was born blind not because of something he had done wrong. He was born blind because of something Jesus wanted to do right.

- This man was not blind because he couldn't see. He couldn't see because he was blind.

- In the same way, we are sinners not because we sin. We sin because we are born sinners.

- We are not born with Christ and then somehow lose him along the way. We are born without Jesus. That is why we must be born again.

As Jesus's response shows us, a place of desperation is a setting for God's transformation.

Believing Is Seeing

Jesus spit on the ground, made mud with his own saliva, and anointed the man's eyes. After the man washed in a pool, as Jesus instructed, he could see.

The old adage says, "Seeing is believing." But in this case, believing is seeing.

That this man went and washed as Jesus instructed means that he believed Jesus. If he hadn't, if this man had said, "I don't know why you're doing this. I don't understand it, and until I do, I'm not going to believe it and I'm not going to obey you," he would have died blind.

But he believed Jesus because he was desperate.

Nobody else had offered a cure. Nobody else had offered a change. Nobody else had offered an opportunity for healing.

If you're living a life of quiet desperation, and if you want your place of desperation to become a setting for God's transformation, believe what Jesus says about you. Believe what Jesus says about himself. And believe what Jesus says he can do through you, in you, and for you.

Receive What Jesus Has

What does a man with blindness need?

Sight.

What does a man in darkness need?

Light.

Jesus, the light of the world, had given this man sight.

You would have thought that everybody would have been happy. You would have thought that the story would have blown up on Facebook and trended on Twitter. You would have thought this man would have been on the front page of the *Jerusalem Times* and on "Good Morning Israel." But instead, one question was repeated over and over.

His neighbors asked, "Is this not the man who used to sit and beg?" (John 9:8). When the man asserted his identity, they demanded, "Then how were your eyes opened?" (v. 10).

The man had been blind from birth and everyone knew it. He might have been around forty years old, so his situation could be verified. But now he can see, and instead of celebration, people want an explanation.

The Pharisees also questioned the man, who recounted the story as it happened.

Then the Jewish religious leaders called the man's parents to grill them. "He's your son. How did this happen?" But Mom and Dad don't want to get involved because they were afraid of getting kicked out of the synagogue. "Ask him yourself," they replied.

When these interrogators call the fellow back to the witness stand, he states, "I am not going to try to explain what I don't know, but I am going to dwell on what I do know. I don't understand completely how this has happened, but you can't deny that it has. I was blind but now I see."

Conceive Who Jesus Is

The man took a risk by being so bold, and the religious leaders threw him out of the synagogue. When Jesus heard that they'd thrown the man out, he found him and asked, "Do you believe in the Son of Man?"

The man replied, "And who is he, sir, that I may believe in him?"

When Jesus revealed himself—it's me!—the man believed and worshiped (John 9:35-38).

Because this man had responded to the *first* light that Jesus had offered him, he now received the *full* light of who Jesus was.

Notice how this man's faith progressed:

- In verse 11, he claims Jesus healed him. The first thing he believes about Jesus is he is a good man.

- When the Pharisees asked him about Jesus, he responds that Jesus is a prophet (v. 17). So he has moved from calling Jesus a good man to a great man because you couldn't pay a person a higher compliment in that day than to call him a prophet.

- But when the Pharisees came back to him a second time and asked about Jesus, he boldly announced, "We know that God does not listen to sinners, but if anyone is a worshiper of God and does his will, God listens to him. Never since the world began has it been heard that anyone opened the eyes of a man born blind. If this man were not from God, he could do nothing" (vv. 31-33).

The man finally confesses that Jesus *must be from God*. He is not just a good man, or even a great man, but he is a godly man. He is the God-man.

When this man responded to the first light that he saw, God gave him more light. As he did with Augustine, God gives us eyes to see him.

This Week's Prayer: *Lord, I am* desperate *for you. Shine your light in my heart so that I may shine as a witness that you are the light of the world.*

This Week's Question: Who did Jesus claim to be, and what am I going to do about it?

18

Spiritually Sovereign

This week's Scriptures:

- Mark 5:1-20
- Mark 1:21-34
- Matthew 12:43-45
- James 4:4-10
- 1 John 3:4-10

Heavenly Rebellion

In one of Jesus's strangest miracles, he uses supernatural power to teach us about supernatural powers.

In Mark 5, Jesus performs a cinema-grade exorcism. A demon-possessed man meets Jesus by the seashore, and Christ casts out the spirits to display his supremacy over the supernatural realm. For many people, this story will seem either irrelevant or downright frightening.

Almost every sport has in it a team that is called the Angels, the Devils, or the Demons. It is almost as if deep down, there's an awareness within all of us that, although invisible to the eye, this world is indeed populated with spiritual beings. The Bible not only confirms this to be true, but doesn't shy away from it in the least.

When God created the world, "[he] saw all that he had made, and it was very good" (Genesis 1:31 NIV). And, of course, "all that he had made" included angels. But since everything was *good*, there were no *evil* angels or demons. And yet in the third chapter of Genesis, Satan, in the form of a serpent, tempts Adam and Eve to disobey God. So somewhere between Genesis 1:31 and Genesis 3:1, something happened: there was a rebellion in the angelic world with many angels turning against God and becoming evil.

As I've studied demons in the Scriptures, I've found three things that will help keep them in proper perspective and help Christians avoid two popular extremes: ignoring them or being obsessed with them.

Jesus's perspective doesn't exist on either pole. He knows they exist. He doesn't allow them to frighten him. And he confronts their presence with the power of God.

Demons Are Real

One of the greatest dangers facing both the church and the world when it comes to demons is not the reality of demons but the fact that we don't believe in them.

A famous German theologian named Rudolf Bultmann made a famous dogmatic statement that expresses the opinion of many: "It is impossible to use electric light and the wireless and to avail ourselves of modern medical and surgical discoveries and at the same time believe in the New Testament world of demons and spirits."[5]

Neither the Gospel writers, nor the apostle Paul, not to mention Jesus Christ himself would agree with that statement.

Throughout Mark's Gospel, he illustrates the reality of demons and the power they can exercise over people. The first miracle recorded in Mark, at the beginning of Jesus's ministry, is the deliverance of a man who'd been possessed by an evil spirit. The spirit shook the man violently and, at Jesus's word, came out of him with a shriek (Mark 1:22-27). The second miracle Mark records includes Jesus ministering to crowds of sick and demon-possessed people (Mark 1:32-34), driving out and silencing demons. Mark says that everywhere Jesus went, he encountered demons: "So he traveled throughout Galilee, preaching in their synagogues and driving out demons" (Mark 1:39 NIV).

God believes in demons, and they believe in God. James 2:19 (NIV) says, "You believe that there is one God. Good! Even the demons believe that—and shudder."

Demons Are Vicious

Later Mark reports, "When Jesus got out of the boat, a man with an impure spirit came from the tombs to meet him" (Mark 5:2 NIV). The word *impure* can also mean "vicious" or "degenerate." This refers primarily to their activity in a physical sense.

The man Jesus encountered who lived in the tombs was off the chain. He'd broken free from the irons on his feet and, night and day, he would cry out and cut himself with stones (Mark 5:3-5). Demons love to cause people to hurt themselves and to hurt others. To put it crudely, demons are bloodthirsty. The psalmist warns:

> They did not destroy the peoples
> as the LORD had commanded them,
> but they mingled with the nations
> and adopted their customs.
> They worshiped their idols,
> which became a snare to them.
> They sacrificed their sons
> and their daughters to false gods.
>
> (Psalm 106:34-37 NIV)

In other words, the Bible says that child sacrifice, the killing of children, is evidence of demonic activity. How much of a demonic influence could be behind the abortion industry that takes the lives of unborn children? (Just a thought.)

Jesus allows the demon (actually many demons) afflicting the man of the tombs to leave him and enter into some pigs that were feeding on a nearby hillside (Mark 5:13).

Though this story sounds downright bizarre to the modern ear, it illustrates the demonic influence on murder and killing and the taking of life. Satan and his demons are in the life-taking business; Jesus is in the life-giving business.

Agents of Sin and Death

By all accounts, Adolf Hitler was responsible for more deaths than any other person who has ever lived. Ultimately, he oversaw some fifty million deaths, including the people he killed and the people who were killed trying to stop him.

Here is what you may not know about Adolf Hitler: He was initiated into Satanism by a man named Dietrich Eckart, one of the seven founders of the Nazi Party. They formed an inner circle known as "the Federal Commissary for Occultism."[6] This was a group of Satanists who practiced black magic to communicate with demons. Many times Adolf Hitler has been called "evil personified" and no wonder.

The impact of demonic activity saturates all manner of murderous activities.

In Mark 5 and elsewhere in the Scriptures, demons are also described as "impure" or "unclean" spirits. This means they are "morally filthy." Demons are involved in sexual sins; there is no question that our culture's fascination with pornography and the worship of sex is due in no small part to the activity of demons.

In Matthew 12:45, demons are also referred to as "evil" or "wicked" spirits. Demons love to encourage false worship of false gods and are behind so many false religions. Demons desire to keep people from coming to the true God, hearing the true Gospel, and placing their faith in the true Christ.

Demons Are Vanquished

I don't want to make the mistake of underestimating or overestimating the power of demons. Demons do have great power. But demons are no match for Jesus or for any follower of Christ in whom Jesus lives.

I've often been asked, "Is it possible for a Christian to be demon-possessed?"

The answer to that question is a decisive *no*. Once the Holy Spirit takes control of a Christian's life, all the demons in hell can't force the Spirit to move out. But followers of Christ can be *demon-influenced*. That is why we need to keep our spiritual guard up, stay in the Word, continue to pray, and not allow ourselves to fall into temptation.

The three most important verses in the Bible, when it comes to the devil and his demons, reveal Christ's power—through Christians!—over demons:

- "Submit yourselves, then, to God. Resist the devil, and he will flee from you" (James 4:7 NIV).

- "You, dear children, are from God and have overcome them, because the one who is in you is greater than the one who is in the world" (1 John 4:4 NIV).

- "And having disarmed the powers and authorities, he made a public spectacle of them, triumphing over them by the cross" (Colossians 2:15 NIV).

When you trust Christ as your Savior and God's Spirit comes to live within you, demons will attack you, but they can never possess or defeat you.

This Week's Prayer: *Lord, give me eyes to see the spiritual realm as you see it, confident that the power of the Holy Spirit is alive in me through Christ.*

This Week's Question: Do you understand you need to rely on God daily in your spiritual warfare?

Jesus, the Storyteller

Spellbinding. Penetrating. Heart-touching. These are fitting adjectives for the stories Jesus told. No less than 35 percent of Jesus's recorded teachings were parables—stories designed to reveal truth—and no one knew how to spin a story better. More than ordinary "once upon a time" tales, Jesus tells earthly stories imbued with both *eternal* and *practical* meanings. The stories Jesus told were not for entertainment but for edification; not for information but for transformation. If you want to know who Jesus was and what he valued, take a plunge into the parables he told.

19

The Seed Sower

This week's Scriptures:

- Matthew 13:1-9
- 1 Peter 1:22-25
- Matthew 9:35-38
- John 4:27-38
- Matthew 28:16-20

A New Measure of Success

Even thinking about sharing one's faith with another makes some people break out in a sweat. You might be one or you might know one. Some feel guilty because they're not searching for the lost. Others feel inadequate to share the Gospel. Others still feel they may make the situation worse, so they decide it's better not to try than to try and fail.

Jesus tells a story that helps us with this (Matthew 13:1-9). A farmer goes out into a field to sow some seed. That seed falls on different types of soil. The quality of the soil determines whether a plant grows or a harvest comes.

The focus of Jesus's parable is on the soils. The sower doesn't change. The seed doesn't change. The only variable determining failure or success is the soil. In other words, evangelism is not dependent on the sower or the seed but on the soil. It is the receptivity of the person that determines whether or not our evangelistic efforts are successful.

Jesus won't do our job—we are to sow. We can't do his job—he is to grow.

We can do our part, but only Christ can reach the heart.

Our Part Is Sowing the Seed

Jesus compared God's Word, and the message of the kingdom, to seed because a seed is productive. The purpose of a seed is to produce fruit.

Do you know how an unbeliever becomes a believer? By having the seed of God's Word planted in his heart. First Peter 1:23 (NIV) says, "For you have been born again, not of perishable seed, but of imperishable, through the living and enduring word of God."

A seed cannot plant itself. It needs a sower. All the seed in the world is useless if the sower does not enter the field and sow it. The farmer cannot do his job sitting in the house. He has to get out to the field. That is why the preaching and the teaching of the Word of God must always be central in everything we do.

Sowing seed was a low-tech operation. The sower would carry seed in the fold of his outer garment, and he would walk along the fields and cast it around. Some would hit hard ground, some rocky ground, some thorny ground, and then some fertile ground. Our responsibility is to just go and sow.

Variety of Soils

Jesus describes the first kind soil as "the path."

In Palestine, people would walk through fields and take the same path each day. As they traveled, they would trample down the grass and the ground would become rock-hard. The seed could not get into this type of soil. It could get *on* the ground, but not *into* the ground.

The second type of soil was rocky soil. Much of Israel is limestone and bedrock that is covered with a thin layer of soil. While the first soil was soil where the seed could not get *in*, this is soil where the seed could not get *down*.

In the thorny soil, however, the seed takes root, but the plant is hindered from growing. It can't get *out*. The Word of God is choked out by financial prosperity and worldly possessions.

These are the people who hear the Word of God and say they want to follow the Son of God, but the golf course, the lake house, the extra money, the bigger paycheck, and the corporate ladder keep getting in the way. Getting and keeping these things is more important than following Jesus.

There is, though, a fourth type of soil. Jesus describes it as a heart receptive to God's Word. This is the heart that bears fruit. Some people will say yes and mean it and bear fruit for God's kingdom.

God's Part Is Producing the Harvest

All a farmer can do is sow seed. Once he does, the harvest is in God's hands. Our job is to sow. God's job is to grow. The key to reaching missing people is not the presentation of the message. It is the penetration of the heart. The presentation is our part. The penetration is God's part.

The equation might look something like this:

Faithful Sharers + Fertile Soil = Fruitful Success

Jesus only asks for you to share what you know and live what you share.

You can sow and have no harvest; the parable proves this. But if you don't sow, there will never be a harvest.

One of the things I do at my church is to challenge folks to ask Christ to give them three people that they could plant their lives into—three people into whom they could sow the seed of his Word—trusting Jesus for the harvest.

The reality is that you don't know the condition of the soil. On the outside, some folks can look hard or shallow or thorny, but you can't know, from the outside, the condition of the soil.

Rock Hard or Pillow Soft?

When I pastored in Mississippi, we rented out the high school football stadium and hosted an event where famous people spoke in order to draw crowds. After the celebrity spoke, I would then preach the Gospel. One night, Terry Bradshaw, quarterback for the Pittsburgh Steelers, gave his testimony.

That night, Pacey Cohen was driving home to commit suicide. He saw this big marquee out front that said, "Hear Terry Bradshaw." Cohen, a Steelers fan, thought to himself, *I'll get one last thrill. I'll go hear my hero and then go home and blow my brains out.*

Three thousand people were in attendance that night, and Pacey was sitting on the top row of the bleachers. He was Jewish and had never heard the Gospel. I was just about to finish the service when I said something I had not planned.

"There is someone here tonight, and it will be your last night on this earth if you do not come give your heart to Jesus Christ," I said. "You will not be alive tomorrow, and you will spend eternity separated from God."

Pacey told me later he would swear in a court of law I was looking him right in the eye. He jumped up and rushed to speak to someone about how to follow Jesus.

After receiving Christ, being baptized, and joining our church, Pacey became a full-time Christian evangelist. God took a rock-hard heart and made it pillow soft. Pacey died of cancer, and his last act was sowing the seed of the Gospel in the heart of his bedside nurse.

You do your job. Jesus will do his.

This Week's Prayer: *Lord, give me boldness to partner with you in evangelism and grant me confidence that you alone are in charge of the harvest.*

This Week's Question: Who are the three people that Christ could be calling *you* to invest in?

20

The Best Boss

This week's Scriptures:

- Matthew 20:1-16
- 1 Timothy 1:12-14
- Romans 5:15-21
- Ephesians 1:3-10
- Romans 11:33-36

The Boss's Generosity

A woman's accounting firm was having a great year. Taxes were due the next day, though, and she wondered if maybe they had taken on too many projects. She called a temp agency, breathed a sigh of relief that they had someone available, and offered to pay $100 for the day. The temp agency agreed.

The next day the temp worker arrived at eight sharp and was put to work closing out projects. At the first coffee break, the boss knew they were in trouble even with this additional worker. She phoned the temp agency again, and they sent another person right over. At lunchtime the lady knew she was *still* in deep trouble. She called the temp agency again and asked for another worker, who they sent over.

Finally, at three o'clock, the boss called back and requested one more worker, who showed up to work the last hour of the day. Then the boss called all the temp workers into her office to thank them profusely. She handed the worker who worked only one hour a crisp one hundred dollar bill, then gave the same to all the other workers.

The first worker hired was furious, demanding, "How could you pay everyone else the same thing you paid me? I put in a full eight hours! That's not fair, and I deserve more."

The accountant stood up, walked around her desk, got nose-to-nose with this man, and said, "I am being unfair? Isn't this my company? Isn't this my money? Maybe your problem isn't your payment but my generosity."

Put in Our Place

You may recognize that this story sounds a lot like the one Jesus told in Matthew 20. It strikes at the heart of what Americans have always been taught: "Equal pay for equal work!" "Demand your rights!" Yet Jesus's telling suggests that those principles don't work in the kingdom of God.

Years ago, I was driving my youngest son to high school, and I asked him to read this parable. Afterward, I said to him, "What stands out more to you than anything else about this story?"

He replied, "It isn't fair."

If this happened today, unions would go on strike. The AFL-CIO would be calling for a federal investigation. The Better Business Bureau would erupt. The air would be thicker with lawsuits than mosquitoes in a marsh.

But Jesus told us in the first verse of Matthew 20 that this is what the kingdom of heaven is like. God's world is not like our world and God's ways are not like our ways.

Parents, the next time one of your kids complains, "That's not fair," just tell him or her, "Neither is God." Yet a proper response to Christ is one of gratitude. This parable teaches us that grace puts us in our place.

God Is Gracious

In Israel, soil was prepared in the spring, vines were pruned in the summer, and grapes were harvested around September.

Almost every village and town had an "agora" or marketplace. Usually there would be one place where common workers came together hoping to be hired for the day. These workers were on the lowest rung of the social ladder, uneducated, and could perform only manual labor. They didn't enjoy the benefits of continual employment. They worked a day at a time. If they didn't work, their families went hungry.

Vineyard owners hired these day laborers at the marketplace, one day at a time, giving them the opportunity to provide for their families.

In the story Jesus told, the first workers, hired around six in the morning, agreed to work for a denarius, minimum wage for a day's work. Later, others were hired. So some workers began at the crack of dawn, working for an agreed upon wage, and some workers came in later not knowing what they were going to receive.

But God doesn't have to hire anyone! God doesn't have to invite anybody to be a part of his family, to be a citizen in his kingdom, or to be a worker in his ministry. He does it because he wants to. His only motivation is grace.

Gratitude for God's Generosity

The owner calls all the workers together to give them their wages. The first surprise is that the people who came to work last are paid first. Normally, people who would come to work first would get paid first, but bucking custom, the owner of the vineyard purposely pays the last workers first because he wants the first workers to know what the last workers get paid.

Amazingly, the workers who were hired at five in the afternoon are paid one denarius—a full day's wage. Word begins to spread among the rest of the workers. Everybody gets out their calculators. The ones hired at the beginning of the day figure they'll get two weeks' pay for one day's work. One man was even heard to say, "I'm going to Disney World!"

But each worker received a denarius.

These early workers can't believe it. They are getting paid exactly the same amount for twelve hours labor that other people got for one! Immediately they scream, "Unfair! We worked longer. We deserve more. We should get bigger paychecks."

Remember, no one is *underpaid* in the parable. This is the cry of the *ungrateful.* They had made the fatal mistake of comparing what they got with what someone else had.

What We Don't Deserve

The man hired at the end of the day came home to his wife and kids and put a denarius down on the table.

His wife hugged him and said, "Thank God you got to work today. We were running out of food and you came through. I know you must be exhausted."

"Not really. I only worked an hour."

The wife looked at him with a puzzled expression. "But that's a full day's wage. How did you get that when you only worked for an hour?"

"Don't ask me. I just know I got hired at five o'clock. I worked one hour. He paid me the same thing he paid the man who came to work at six this morning."

The wife looked at him and said, "You got what you didn't deserve."

With a broad smile on his face, the man said, "Don't we all?"

He seemed to know something about the master's grace, didn't he? After working enough days for stingy bosses, he had finally encountered a master who was gracious and generous.

Look at everything you have. Not just materially but relationally, socially, financially, and even physically and realize that *it is all just grace.*

This Week's Prayer: *Lord, give me a heart that is a reflection of your own generous heart! Let me live out the abundance of your gracious Gospel of good news.*

This Week's Question: Where do you find yourself in this story, and how is Jesus speaking to you through it?

21

The Eye Opener

This week's Scriptures:

- Luke 10:25-37
- James 2:14-17
- Luke 6:32-36
- Colossians 3:12-17
- Hebrews 13:1-3

A Surprising Neighbor

After disembarking a plane during a layover in Iran, an American businessman stopped by the bathroom. When he finished washing his hands, he looked down to realize his bag had been stolen. His wallet, cell phone, and passport were inside.

He was traveling with a coworker, but his supposed friend said he couldn't stay around and help. His wife had planned an important party, and he had to get on the next flight and get back home.

Frantic, the businessman approached the airline desk and asked for help. The line was backed up, and the airline employee said, "Sir, I am sorry. There is nothing I can do to help you. I've got to help these other people."

After curling up on an airport seat to rest, he looked up to see a man in traditional Muslim dress standing next to his wife in a full burka. There was a kindness in the man's eyes when he said, "Sir, are you all right? How can I help?"

The man and his wife proceeded to treat the American to dinner, drive him to the American Embassy, help him call his family, and return him to the airport. As he stepped out of their car, the wife said, "Sir, we think you will need this." She handed him a roll of cash in the exact amount he needed to pay for his return trip home.

A Trick Question

In Luke 10, a lawyer asks Jesus how to inherit eternal life. This question is a test and a trap.

Instead of answering the lawyer's question, Jesus lets him answer it. "You're an expert on the law, so you tell me what the law says." The lawyer answers correctly (love God and your neighbor), receives an *A*, but he realizes that he had fallen into a trap he had set himself.

He knows he's supposed to love his neighbor with his heart, soul, mind, and strength, but puts on the brakes and says, "Whoa, wait a minute! Who is my neighbor?"

Like any good lawyer, he is looking for a loophole. His question assumes there are two categories of people: neighbors and nonneighbors. As a good first-century Jew, he expects Jesus to give him a list of neighbors that included Pharisees, Sadducees, and certainly synagogue- and temple-attending Jews, but not Gentiles, and *certainly* not Samaritans!

This know-it-all assumed the answer would be, "Your neighbors are people who are just like you."

But Jesus's answer couldn't have been further from what the lawyer expected.

Friend in Need

I got to travel the Jericho Road only once. It has since been closed, declared too dangerous to travel because of how steep it is and how treacherous it is to navigate.

The Jericho Road is seventeen miles long and it drops from Jerusalem, which is twenty-seven hundred feet above sea level, to Jericho, which is eight hundred feet below sea level. In other words, that desert road drops a little over two hundred feet every mile.

Worse, in Jesus's day, bandits and robbers roamed the region, making it one of the most crime-ridden areas in Israel. Bible scholars estimate there were at least twelve thousand thieves scattered throughout the Judean wilderness between Jerusalem and Jericho. Imagine lawless gangs roaming around like packs of wild dogs attacking innocent victims, beating them, and stealing their valuables. Traveling this road was so dangerous that the ancients nicknamed it "The Way of Blood."

Jesus tells about one victim—robbed, beaten, and left half dead. There is a lot we don't know about this man, but we do know he is a man in need. You may recall the popular saying, "A friend in need is a friend indeed." Jesus shows us the only two ways we will always respond to people in need.

Rationalize the Situation in Your Mind

When Jesus mentions a priest passing by in this story, optimism rises in the hearts of his audience. The priest is a holy man, a righteous man, and a religious man. Surely he will be the first one to help. But the moment he saw the injured man, he passed by on the other side.

The wounded man could have been dead. If he was, and the priest had touched him, he would have become ceremonially defiled. He would have had to go back to Jerusalem and undergone a weeklong ceremonial cleansing. In addition, what if other robbers were in the area?

Then a Levite comes by. This doesn't mean much to modern readers, but ancient hearers would know that a Levite was a royal blue blood. He belonged to the tribe of Levi, and he was an assistant to the priest. He might even have been an assistant to *this* priest. Maybe knowing that the priest had passed by and had done nothing, he thought maybe the priest knew something he didn't, and he shouldn't do anything either. *Since he didn't get involved, why should I get involved?*

Amazingly, the two people you were sure would have stopped to help this man didn't. Jesus subtly shows they were no better than the thieves who beat and robbed this man and left him for dead.

The priest and the Levite were bad neighbors because they refused to be good neighbors.

Respond to the Situation with Your Heart

Jesus continues his story, "But a Samaritan, as he journeyed, came to where he was, and when he saw him, he had compassion."

To a first-century Jew, the only good Samaritan was a dead Samaritan. No class or race of people was hated more by the Jewish people than Samaritans. They were publicly cursed in the synagogue and were excluded from temple worship. Prayers would be offered every day begging God to keep them out of heaven.

Why? Pure racism.

What this Samaritan does is nothing short of amazing. He uses all his available resources—oil, wine, personal clothing, his animal, time, energy, and money—to give this Jewish man the best care possible.

The Samaritan risks his own life by taking this wounded man to an inn in Jewish territory. Then, to top it off, the Samaritan gives the innkeeper enough money to cover the man's food and lodging for several days, then promises to come back and pay anything else the man owes. This is important, because any person who could not pay their bill could be sold as a slave by the innkeepers in order to get full payment for a debt.

When Jesus asks which man proved to be a good neighbor, the lawyer couldn't even spit out the word *Samaritan*. Instead, he mumbles, "The one who showed him mercy."

What made this Samaritan so special was not the color of his skin but the compassion in his heart. No law will ever make you be a good neighbor, but real love can't keep you from being a good neighbor.

A neighbor is not defined by color or creed; a neighbor is defined by nearest need.

This Week's Prayer: *Lord, I admit that I am tempted to pass by those who suffer. Give me courage to recognize a "neighbor" in the face of those in need.*

This Week's Question: Are the ways you've behaved toward those in need like the religious ones who would not pause to help?

22

The Divine Auditor

This week's Scriptures:

- Matthew 25:14-30
- Romans 12:3-8
- 1 Corinthians 12:1-11
- 1 Corinthians 12:12-31
- Ephesians 4:1-16

A Kingdom Melody

They are in every Broadway musical. They are at every college football game. They are at every presidential inauguration. They spend every day of the year with Mickey, Minnie, Goofy, and Donald at Disney World.

And though they're most likely not the reason you'd buy a ticket for admission, their absence at any of these events would be noticeable.

I'm talking about bands and orchestras.

If you study famous musicians that have learned to play any musical instrument with skill, you will find that they often learned their craft and honed their skill by playing in a band or an orchestra. That's because certain skills—learning to blend with other instruments, keeping up to tempo, learning to play louder or softer, following a conductor's lead—can be learned only by playing in a band or orchestra.

What is true of a band or an orchestra is even truer of a community of believers.

Jesus told a parable about people playing their parts and how important that is to the church and to God's kingdom. Not everyone plays the same instrument and not everyone has the same part. Some instruments are louder than others and some parts are bigger than others. It's not how much you have that matters to Jesus; it's what you do with what you have that matters to him.

A God-Given Opportunity to Play Our Parts

To help us grasp the value of using what we have, Jesus tells a story in Matthew 25 about a master, prepping to go out of town, who entrusts his property to his servants.

The key word is *entrusted*. This man had taken his property, his money, and had entrusted it to others to use productively and profitably. Each servant had been given an opportunity to show what he could do with this man's investment.

As it is with us, not everyone had been given equal amounts of what Jesus called "talents." Different people are born into different situations and have different gifts and abilities. We think of a talent as an ability, but that is not what the word means here. A talent, in the ancient world, was a measure of money. The value of one talent was equal to twenty years of wages for an average worker. Even though each man had been given different amounts, in the eyes of the master every man had been given a significant amount. Don't miss this: there are no unimportant instruments in God's orchestra. There are no *little talents* in God's kingdom.

These talents were different in amount, but they were the same in source. They had all been given by the master.

A God-Given Responsibility to Play Our Parts

Each servant in this story had been given some ability. Not the *same* ability, but *some* ability. Every ability is an opportunity. And every opportunity carries with it the responsibility to seize that opportunity, to use that ability for the glory of God.

God has given every one of us certain abilities, unique personalities, and personal opportunities that he expects us to leverage for his glory and for the good of others. Just like money, they are to be invested.

Some of the servants understood that, but some of the servants didn't.

> "He who had received the five talents went at once and traded with them, and he made five talents more. So also he who had the two talents made two talents more. But he who had received the one talent went and dug in the ground and hid his master's money" (Matthew 25:16-18).

Jesus's story identifies what success means in the eyes of God: success is exercising responsibility, seizing every opportunity, and using your abilities for the glory of God and the good of others. What is important to God is not what ability he has given you but how you use it.

A God-Given Accountability to Play Our Parts

Jesus continues to reveal that what's important to God is what you do with what you've been given. Even though one man made five more talents, where the other man only made two more, they were both equally rewarded. It didn't matter who started out with the most. It didn't matter who ended up with the most. What mattered was what they did with what they had.

In a way, I wish that was where the story ended. The rest of the story makes so many of us uncomfortable, and it is why a lot of people don't like this parable.

While the first two servants brought effort, the third servant brought an excuse. It is interesting that when Jesus asked the two faithful servants what they did with their talents, they just said, "We took the talents you gave us and made more talents." The unfaithful servant took forty-two words to say, "I didn't do anything."

This man had buried his talent! He didn't even put it in the bank. He didn't even try to draw any interest.

All Christ wants every one of us to do is play our part. Jesus does not expect the same results, but he does expect the same effort. He never compares you with anyone else. He compares you only with you. Jesus doesn't look at what you have. He looks only at what you do with what you have.

Every Player Matters

If you know anything about football, you know that the most easily identifiable player on any football team and the most valuable player to that team is the quarterback. He is the "field general" who calls the plays, runs the offense, and is primarily responsible for whether or not his team scores points. That is why by far the highest paid position in the NFL is quarterback.

Can you guess what position the second-highest paid player in the NFL plays? No, it isn't running back. No, it isn't wide receiver. No, it isn't any player on defense. The second-highest paid player in the NFL is the left offensive tackle. Do you know why? Because he protects the blind side of the quarterback, which is where the quarterback, and therefore the offense, and therefore the team, is most vulnerable.

Take any Super Bowl winning team of the last several years, and any fan can name the quarterback, but the only ones who can name the left tackle are his wife and his mother. Yet, he played on a championship team because he played his part.

When you play yours, you will stand before the God who made you, and he will say, "Well done, good and faithful servant."

This Week's Prayer: *Lord, teach me to be a good steward of the talents you've given to me. Grant me the wisdom to use them wisely and the courage to share them freely.*

This Week's Question: What are the particular talents—gifts, resources, treasures, abilities—that God has entrusted only to *you*?

23

A Better Financial Planner

This week's Scriptures:

- Luke 12:13-21
- Romans 12:9-13
- 2 Corinthians 9:6-15
- 1 Timothy 6:6-10
- James 2:1-7

How Do You See Your Wealth?

If I told you that this week's reflections were just for people who were rich, you might just close this book. Your first response might be, "I'm not rich, so I'll just go play Words With Friends." Or maybe you'd start daydreaming about the kind of person who would keep reading: the nineteen-year-old millionaire entrepreneur or the ninety-one-year-old retired business mogul.

Guess what? You are richer than you think.

The median income in the United States is $50,064. That means that if your household is in that ballpark, you are in the top 0.98 percent richest people in the world.

And if you make minimum wage, around $15,000 to $20,000 a year—hardly enough for rent, food, and clothing—you are still in the top 12.2 percent richest people in the world.

We need only three things to live: shelter, food, and clothing. Everything else is wealth. As you think about the wealth that you have—the closets full of clothes and shoes, the attic and the basement full of stuff you bought that's gathering dust—remember that the way you see your wealth determines your spiritual health.

What I'm asking you to consider is this: Since everything must go, because one day you will go, where will everything go before you do?

Secret Wanting

One of the most fascinating biographies I've ever read was of John D. Rockefeller. At the turn of the twentieth century, he was the only billionaire in the world. He owned Standard Oil, which at the time was the only major oil refinery on the planet.

Someone asked Mr. Rockefeller one time, "How much money is enough?"

He famously replied, "Just a little bit more. Just a little bit more."

Covetousness is a disease that is contagious and easily caught. The cause of it is one word: *more*. The greatest cause of obesity is eating more than one should. The top cause for financial problems is spending more than one should. We've got attics and basements and garages stored with stuff because we all have more and want more than we need.

Covetousness is one sin you can keep a secret and nobody notices. You could be a covetous person twenty-four hours a day and nobody but you would ever know it.

The man in the parable Jesus tells in Luke 12 was already a rich man. He had more than he needed, but he wanted more than he had.

Be Content with What You Have

Jesus begins by warning "Be on your guard against all covetousness," or "Be in control of what you want." Then he introduces us to a man who was both rich and a fool. He was foolishly rich and richly foolish. This farmer was not a fool because he was rich. He was not a fool because he was prosperous and successful. The Bible nowhere ever condemns well-earned, well-deserved financial prosperity.

He was a fool because he misunderstood where his wealth had come from. If you were to ask him where his wealth had come from, he would have said something like, "I worked for it and I earned it. I plowed the fields. I planted the grain. I tended the soil and I gathered the harvest." That is what it looked like on the surface, but Jesus describes it differently: "The land of a rich man produced plentifully" (Luke 12:16).

Jesus didn't say, "A certain man worked hard and accumulated a great fortune." He said, "It was the land that produced plentifully." In other words, God had given the farmer the land. God had sent the rain and the sun. God had used the process he'd created to turn the soil and the seed into a harvest. God had given him his money. And the man saw his money, his land, and his income as what he earned rather than what God had given.

Foolish Thinking

This man was blind. He couldn't see the God who gave him his wealth, and he couldn't see others who needed some of his wealth. Greed had pulled the shades of selfishness over his eyes and had coated his heart in the concrete of covetousness.

His attitude was, "I've got more stuff, so I guess I need more storage." Do you know why? He thought everything that came to him was for him.

Then, for the first and only time in any parable that Jesus ever told, God himself makes an appearance and he speaks.

> "But God said to him, 'Fool! This night your soul is required of you, and the things you have prepared, whose will they be?'" (Luke 12:20).

This man thought his security was in his money. This man thought he had many years left, but he didn't have another day!

Do you know why this man was a fool? Can I give you the bottom line? He was a fool for two reasons: Everything he had he thought he owned, but he didn't. And he thought he could keep it all, but he couldn't.

Be Conscious of Where You Are Going

Most people think that what they have is for them. But if you understand that everything you have comes *from* him and is *for* him, you will handle your finances completely differently.

I invite you to take an hour's wage, based on your salary, and give it to somebody else. If you donated just one hour's salary, this is what you could do:

- $8 could buy *you* fifteen organic apples, or it could provide twenty-five fruit trees for farmers in Honduras to grow and sell fruit at their local market.

- $30 could buy *you* a DVD boxed set, or it could supply a first-aid kit for a village in Haiti.

- $73 could buy *you* a new mobile phone, or it could resource a new mobile health clinic to care for AIDS orphans in Uganda.

- $2400 could buy *you* a high-definition TV, or it could provide schooling for an entire generation of school children in an Angolan village.

The only cure for covetousness, the only solution for selfishness, and the only medicine for materialism is giving to those who need what you have by becoming rich toward God. That is what Jesus did for us by dying for our sins, and that is what we can do for others in turn. If Jesus were a rich man, that is what he would do.

This Week's Prayer: *Lord, thank you for meeting my needs. I agree that what is mine is yours—guide me as I give to those who need what I have.*

This Week's Question: How is Jesus calling you to use what you have to meet others' needs today?

24

The God of Tomorrow

> **This week's Scriptures:**
>
> - Luke 16:1-13
> - Romans 14:10-12
> - Psalm 39:4-7
> - Luke 12:35-40
> - 1 Timothy 6:6-11

Preparing for Tomorrow

When the phone rang, the man's stomach turned. He'd been dreading this call: "Sir, I'm calling from the bank to let you know we're foreclosing on your home. You'll be evicted in one week."

The man begged, "I haven't been able to find work since I was laid off, and I have nowhere to take my wife and children."

"Sir, I'm sorry. There's nothing I can do."

He quickly kicked into survival mode. Grabbing his tools, he began dismantling the light fixtures and removing the nonessential appliances. The next day, he dragged them into his yard and sold them in a yard sale. Then he went to work removing his air-conditioning units, which he promptly sold for a handsome price. He even sold the lightbulbs, shutters, windows, toilets, and the hot-water heater.

The day the bank official came to evict them, the family had already left. They'd taken the money they'd gathered, rented an apartment, and filled it with groceries for a month.

When the banker relayed the story to his wife, he mused, "In a way, I kind of admire him."

"What!" she said. "How can you admire someone like that?"

"Well, he did what he could with what he had today to prepare for tomorrow."

Money Lovers

This, of course, is a retelling of a parable Jesus told (Luke 16). On the surface, Jesus's story appears to be about an account manager who cheated his boss and is commended by Jesus for being a liar and a thief. It's what makes this parable both difficult and fascinating.

It's a story about money, something Jesus taught more about than any other topic—not because *he* was obsessed with it, but because he knew *we* would be obsessed with it.

He told this parable, in part, because of a special group in the crowd that was listening to it: "The Pharisees, who were lovers of money, heard all these things, and they ridiculed him" (Luke 16:14).

This parable is directed especially to people who love money. So…that's most of us.

As you consider everything that you have—your money, your house, your car, your clothes, real estate, stocks, bonds, your 401(k)—consider this: one day you will have to give an account for your accounts, so you had better account for your accounts wisely.

Accountable for the Management of What We Have

This story, with a surprise twist and a shocking ending, revolves around a manager. The Greek word for *manager* actually comes from two words. One word meaning "house" and the other word meaning "to manage." This person is a "house-manager."

In the first century, rich people would often appoint managers called "stewards." They were given the full power of attorney to act in the name of the master. They controlled all the assets and represented the master in every business transaction.

There were two things this manager knew. First, not a dime of what he managed belonged to him. Second, he was being watched and would have to give an account for what he did with what he had.

Somehow the rich man in Jesus's parable had gotten word that his manager had been mismanaging his money. So he called the manager in and fired him on the spot.

Just like this manager, one day we will have to give an account for our accounts. I don't mean just our money but our lives. Romans 14:12 says,

"So then each of us will give an account of himself to God" (Romans 14:12).

A Shrewd Dude

The debts owed to this rich man were huge. One guy owed olive oil worth three-years' wages for an average worker, and another owed wheat worth seven-and-a-half-years' wages!

The going interest rate on oil that was borrowed was 100 percent, and the interest on borrowed wheat was 25 percent—so the manager reduces what is owed by exactly the amount of the interest that was charged. In other words, the manager transforms these debts into interest-free loans.

Imagine someone comes to your door, tears up your mortgage, and says you'll never pay interest again, only principle. You think you and that guy might become best buddies?

But these clients assumed that the manager was doing this at the request of the master. So the word in town spread about this generous owner, who'd been known as a penny-pincher. Now he was the hero of the town!

And the master *commended* him.

This owner could have gone to the village and said that the reductions weren't authorized and that they had to pay their amounts in full. But these people would never do business with him again. The owner did the only thing he could do: he kept his mouth shut and accepted all the slaps on the back, though they were expensive slaps.

The owner did not commend the steward for *what* he had done, but for *how* he had done it. He said, "You are a shrewd dude." He had used what the owner had given him today to make sure he would be taken care of tomorrow.

Investments that Last

Willard Cantelon, in his book *The Day the Dollar Dies*, tells the story of a German mother who wanted to help build a Bible school outside the city of Frankfurt, which had been destroyed after the war. All during the war she had held her money with pride and tenderness, hoarding it, guarding it, stashing it away because one day she would invest it in a worthy cause.

The day that she was going to take her money and use it to build that school, the German mark had been cancelled by the government. That Sunday, in June of 1948, a staggering number of Germans committed suicide. Millions had lost their savings. Like this woman, they had failed to exchange their money for something that would survive the economic collapse.

One day, everything you have or think you have will be gone. It will either be lost somehow before you die, or certainly gone after you die. One day you are going to lose it, so use it today to get ready for tomorrow.

That is exactly what Jesus did when he died on the cross and was raised from the dead. He invested the life that he lived those thirty-three years on earth, so we could get ready for the tomorrow of eternity.

Take everything you have, everything you are, and give it to Christ today so you will be ready for tomorrow.

This Week's Prayer: *Lord, all that I have is yours. Teach me to be a wise steward with what belongs to you and invest in your eternal kingdom.*

This Week's Question: Do your eternal investments with your *life* outweigh your financial ones?

25

The Life of the Party

This week's Scriptures:

- Luke 15:1-10
- 2 Peter 3:8-10
- 2 Timothy 2:22-26

- Luke 5:27-32
- Ezekiel 34:11-16

Unlikely Companions

There were always two types of people around Jesus: the rebellious crowd and the religious crowd. Today some would identify these as the "wrong" crowd and the "right" crowd. The rebellious crowd might include drug addicts, ex-cons, and gang members. The religious crowd would, most certainly, include Christians dressed to the nines in their Sunday best. A lot of church people are more like the Pharisees than they'd care to admit. And because the Pharisees considered themselves the "right" crowd, it drove them *nuts* that Jesus hung around with the "wrong" crowd (Luke 15:1-2).

The Pharisees didn't understand why Jesus—someone who claimed to be the Son of God—hung around with sinners because they didn't see sinners the way God does. They saw sinners as *losers*, but God sees sinners as *lost*.

To capture the holy imagination of those with hardened hearts, Jesus discovered that everybody—he, sinners, and even the Pharisees—could agree that if a sheep is lost, the shepherd of that sheep is going to look for it. Good shepherds don't care about *some* of the flock or even *most* of the flock. They care about *all* of the flock. And that becomes most evident when one sheep gets lost.

A Lost Sheep

A young couple was shopping at the mall with their two-year-old, Jimmy, when the husband stopped at a store to try on a pair of pants. Jimmy was sitting in a stroller, his diaper bag and his mother's purse hanging off the handles.

When the husband emerged from the dressing room, he looked at his wife and asked, "Where's Jimmy?"

The pair scanned the area, searching for their son, but Jimmy, the stroller, the purse, and the diaper bag were gone! They frantically dashed around the store, but couldn't find Jimmy anywhere. When they asked a salesperson if she'd seen a little boy and a stroller, her reply was surprisingly nonchalant.

"Yes," she said. "He just pushed the stroller out the door about two minutes ago."

"Why didn't you stop him?" the father demanded.

"He wasn't my kid."

The couple ran out into the mall, eyes darting in every direction, but they couldn't find their son. Instinctively, perhaps, they turned to the right, walked up two flights of steps, and headed for the toy store.

Glancing into the window, the couple spotted their son. Entirely content, Jimmy was sitting in a little red toy car, next to the family's stroller, waving at his parents through the window.

On the verge of breaking down, the father gulped a deep breath to regain his composure. Overwhelmed with relief, the couple experienced deep joy.

This isn't a fictional story or even the story of a stranger. It's a true story about my son James! In those harrowing moments, I came to understand the heart of Jesus who is the *finder* of the lost.

My son James wasn't a loser, he was *lost*.

Family and Not-Yet-Family

As a follower of Jesus Christ, when you view a person who is far from God the same way that you see a child who is lost, your attitude and priorities toward them will change completely. I experienced a powerful rush of joy when I was finally reunited with my son, and God's exuberance when the lost are found is even greater than his celebration of those who are already "in the family."

What was true of my son James is true of sheep: the one that's lost doesn't even realize it's lost! Not only did James not *know* he was lost, he didn't *care* that he was lost. The shepherd has to keep careful watch over the flock because sheep just naturally wander away. And when they do, they don't return because they neither realize they are lost nor are smart enough to find their way back. A person far from Jesus is lost. He is like a blind man in a dark room looking for a black cat that is not there.

Did you notice what the shepherd in Jesus's story did? He left the ninety-nine sheep to fend for themselves, and he went to look for the one sheep that had wandered off. What made that sheep so valuable was the love and concern of the one who had lost it.

Jesus doesn't love us because we are valuable; we are valuable because Jesus loves us.

A Helpless Wanderer Found

If you're a parent, you have had or will have the experience of losing track of your child. (Kids are like ninjas—they disappear right before your eyes!) When you do, catch your breath and know that, in a way you never would have chosen, you have encountered the heart and mind of God.

I recently read a story about a little girl who lived at the edge of a big forest. One day she wandered off into the woods to explore, but soon lost her bearings, unable to find her way back home. As darkness descended, fear gripped her heart. She screamed and cried and wept until finally she just lay down and slept.

Her father, hoarse from calling out her name, had been searching for several hours when he discovered the girl lying on a patch of grass. Calling out to her, he dashed to the girl's side as quickly as he could.

The little girl woke up, jumped into his arms, hugged and kissed him, and said, "Daddy, I'm so glad I found you!"

This is our story too. We don't find Jesus; he finds us. And Jesus finds us because he is always looking for us.

Cause for Great Rejoicing

Upon finding his lost sheep, the shepherd in Jesus's story did something that would have left the crowds scratching their heads. He threw a party, inviting his friends and neighbors, "Rejoice with me!"

Now imagine that these guests show up but have no idea what they are celebrating. Once everyone has arrived, before they sit down to eat and drink, the host points to this one little lamb and says, "That sheep was lost, but now it is found. Let's party!"

The deepest desire of Jesus's heart is that the lost be found. In what would have felt like a punch in the gut to the self-righteous Pharisees listening in, Jesus announces, "I tell you, there will be more joy in heaven over one sinner who repents than over ninety-nine righteous persons who need no repentance" (Luke 15:7). Every time one person repents, every time one person surrenders their life to Jesus Christ, every time one lost person is found, God says, "It's party time!"

Can you imagine the angels up in heaven as they gaze upon God? All of a sudden God begins to shout, dance, and rejoice. He breaks out the food and the drink. One angel says, "There he goes again. Somebody else just repented. Somebody else just got found. Somebody else just surrendered to Jesus."

Because lost people matter to Jesus, they matter to us. And as we pursue the lost with the love of Christ, heaven rejoices.

This Week's Prayer: *Lord, kindle in my heart your passion for the lost. Give me eyes to see as you see and the will to pursue and invite them into the celebration that awaits them.*

This Week's Question: Do you share the Shepherd's passion to pursue the one who is lost?

26

A Hospitable Host

This week's Scriptures:

- Luke 14:12-24
- John 6:35-40
- Matthew 11:25-30

- Isaiah 55:1-5
- Revelation 19:6-9

An Offer Not to Be Refused

Imagine this: U2 has just made an announcement they are splitting up. They'll perform one last farewell concert at Madison Square Garden in New York City. One night only.

A popular DJ in Manhattan gets five free tickets with backstage passes, but company policy strictly prohibits him from using them. For days he announces a big on-air giveaway, offering the tickets to the one-hundredth caller. He expects the phone lines to be jammed.

When the magic day and hour arrive, not one person calls.

Now time is ticking. The concert is only a few hours away, so the DJ begins calling his friends. One buddy said he had to take his child to soccer practice. Another friend said he and his wife usually went grocery shopping that night. Another man said he would like to, but he was going to paint his bathroom instead.

In complete disbelief, the DJ slams the phone down, walks out into the city street, and finds five homeless men sitting in front of the studio.

"Hey, guys! I'd like to invite you an all-inclusive night at the arena across the street. It's U2's final concert. I've got five tickets with backstage passes and an all-you-can-eat buffet. Are you guys interested?"

At first, the stunned men are absolutely speechless. Then they jump to their feet, happily receive the tickets, and enter the arena to enjoy front row seats at U2's last, epic concert.

An Offer Refused

Jesus wanted us to know that his Father's kingdom is *like that*.

Instead of a concert, in Luke 14 Jesus describes a host inviting people to a meal. It's a Sabbath Day, and Jesus is dining at the house of a ruler of the Pharisees, who were watching him carefully. They were trying to trap him by getting him involved in a debate that he could not win.

To cut the tension, one of the men chimed in, "Blessed is everyone who will eat bread in the kingdom of God!" (Luke 14:15).

This man was not just making a statement; he was making an assumption. He was saying that he and all his pharisaical buddies would surely have a place at God's table in the kingdom of God.

But what the Pharisees failed to realize was that the kingdom of God was not something that they were to be looking for *tomorrow*, it was already present in Jesus.

He'd invited them to follow him. He'd invited them to fellowship with him. Feeling they'd already earned their spot in the kingdom, they turned his invitation down.

Have I Heard God's Invitation to Me?

Jesus is the host of the big party, inviting everyone to be a part of his kingdom and to have a seat at his table. The meal has been prepared. It is hot and ready to eat.

In the Middle East there were actually *two* invitations that were sent out for a banquet. There was an invitation that would be sent out far enough ahead of the banquet so that people could put the date on their calendar. They would know the day of the banquet, but they wouldn't know the exact hour. These invitations were sent with an RSVP. Everybody would have to let the host know that they were coming so the host would know how much meat to cook, how much bread to bake, and how much wine to serve.

Just before the feast began, the host would send out his servants to give the second invitation for guests to come. The first invitation had already been given. The guests had already agreed to come, and now they needed to take their places at the table.

And the feast they'd enjoy was *free*.

Have I Honored God's Invitation to Me?

The door was open, the host was waiting, and the silverware and china were in place. The dishes were filled to overflowing with meats, vegetables, and fruits. The goblets were filled with wine.

The host scanned the horizon, looking for his guests, but no one showed up because they'd all made excuses. Not even good excuses, either!

The first one said he bought a field and had to go see it. But to buy or sell good cropland was a long exacting process that would stretch over months and sometimes even years. Because Israel has a lot of desert land, as well as some land suitable for farming, the farmer had no doubt learned everything he could about this land to make sure he could make money off it.

The next guest had bought five yoke of oxen. Normally, one man could work only one yoke, but this man had bought *five*. He wasn't a small-time farmer. This was a big-time rancher, probably owning close to one-hundred acres. No rancher would have bought such valuable animals without looking at them.

A third guest used the weak excuse of a recent marriage. Yet what woman doesn't like to dress up for a party! But like the others, this man didn't go to the banquet because he didn't want to go to the banquet.

But there is *no* legitimate excuse to reject God's invitation to be a part of his family or to have a place at his table. To reject God's gracious invitation dishonors the One who loved you enough to send his Son to die for you.

Have I Heeded God's Invitation to Me?

The host is obviously a rich man. But when his guests refuse his offer, he goes to the down and out. This time there was not a unanimous no, but a unanimous yes.

Can you imagine how thrilled they would be to receive this invitation? I can.

Once former president George H.W. Bush was in Atlanta, and I was invited to bring my sons to a fund-raising dinner for a candidate who was running for election. I was told we would be sitting at the table with the former president.

I didn't say, "I wish I could, but I must go to Kroger's and shop."

I didn't even say, "Sorry, but I've got a golf match that day."

I said, "I'll be there."

I received that invitation. I honored that invitation. I heeded that invitation. Now my sons and I have a memory we will never forget.

We've all been given a far greater invitation to sit at the table of the Creator of the universe, the King of kings and the Lord of lords, and to enjoy his presence forever.

This Week's Prayer: *Thank you, Lord, that you've invited me to feast in your presence at your table. Quicken my heart that I might always be ready to say yes when you call.*

This Week's Question: When Jesus called you, did you drop everything to show up at his banquet? Do you today?

27

The Object of Our Worship

This week's Scriptures:

- Luke 18:9-14
- Matthew 7:14-23
- Matthew 7:1-5
- Isaiah 6:1-7
- Luke 5:1-11

A Tale of Two Men

A minister lives with his family in a comfortable gated neighborhood. At the front of the house are bay windows where the pastor kneels to pray every morning, hoping that his neighbors will see him, because he wants to be a witness.

The minister says, "Dear God, I am so grateful for who I am and what I have. I am so grateful that, unlike so many people, I have never had a drink. I've never smoked. I've never used profanity. I have been faithful to my wife and a good father to my children. I am just thankful I am not like so many people out there who live such terrible lifestyles, and I never will be."

On the other side of town, where half the homes are boarded up, is a dark house, without electricity. It smells of urine and vomit. Used syringes were scattered across the floor.

In the upstairs room, a man sits in front of a coffee table where a line of cocaine has been sprinkled and scraped. Caught in the grip of addiction, he drops to his knees to begin snorting another line, when a flood of conviction breaks through the dam of his heart.

Instead of reaching for the syringe, he looks up to heaven and says, "O God, I am the least worthy person to talk to you. I have made terrible choices, and I have suffered the consequences. God, would you please have mercy on me?"

Two houses. Two men. Two prayers.

One question: In God's eyes, who do you think got up off their knees justified?

This Story May Be for You

Jesus tells a story in Luke 18 about two men in a similar situation, but with a surprising twist. One man was convinced for the wrong reason he was right with God, but he was wrong. One man was convinced for the right reasons he was wrong with God, and he got right.

Jeff Foxworthy has become famous for identifying rednecks. To go into Foxworthy mode, "You just might be in this parable if..." any of the following things are true about you:

- Do you ever look at people who don't go to church and think you are better than they are, because you do go to church?
- Do you ever look at people who drink and think that you are better than they are, because you don't?
- Do you ever look at someone who may be living in sexual sin and thank God, because you aren't?

If so, Jesus is talking to you.

When you look up to God, you will never look down on others.

One man in Jesus's story was rejected by God, and the other was accepted. Why? Because of how they looked at themselves.

Don't Bother Comparing

In the first century, there were two services every day in the temple when lambs were sacrificed and an atonement was made for sin. The early service started at sunup and the late service started at three o'clock. Each service began outside the sanctuary, at the altar, where the sacrifice for sins would take place. Trumpets would sound, cymbals would clang, and someone would read a psalm. The priest would then enter the outer part of the sanctuary where he would offer incense and trim the lamps. When he left, anybody could offer prayers to God.

In first-century Judaism, the Pharisee was the Eagle Scout. If anybody was okay with God, one might reason, it must be the Pharisees.

"Pharisee" has a negative connotation today, but not so two thousand years ago. You could have taken a vote and any Pharisee would have overwhelmingly been chosen as the one who would have been most likely to know God, meet God, and be right with God.

The Pharisee in Jesus's story compares himself with those he thought were beneath him: extortionists, adulterers, and tax collectors. He let God know that, unlike those slackers, he fasted more than was required and he tithed on more of his property than he was required (Luke 18:12). He thought he could look up to God and look down on others. C.S. Lewis wisely said, "A proud man is always looking down on things and people; but as long as you are looking down you can't see anything that is above you."

See Yourself Correctly

These two men could not be more different. A Pharisee was regarded as being as different from a tax collector as the pope would be from a pimp. Not only did a tax collector not give any money to the temple, but he stole from the people who went there.

We are told that he "stood far off." He was expected to. No one would have anything to do with him. Where the Pharisee would stand in the center of the court, the tax collector slipped in the back, standing in the shadows (Luke 18:13).

This man is seeing himself correctly. Do you know why? You will see yourself correctly only when you see God correctly. When you see God correctly you will understand that only God is perfect and no one else is.

When this man says, "Be merciful to me," he doesn't use the normal word for "mercy." The word here goes back to the Hebrew word *kippur*, which means "atonement," as in Yom Kippur, which means "the Day of Atonement." The word *atonement* means "to cover." What this man said was, "God, I am admitting what you already know is true about me. I am a sinful man with a sinful heart. God, will you cover for me?" That is all that God needed and wanted to hear from either one.

See Yourself Clearly

One man said he was innocent, but he went home guilty. One man said he was guilty, but he went home innocent.

I imagine the conversation in the temple court that day might have gone differently.

That Pharisee should have walked over to the tax collector and said something like, "What are you doing here? I've not seen you before."

"You know I am a tax collector and I rip people off for a living. God has finally shown me what I am and who I am, and I am embarrassed to be here, but I've realized I need God to have mercy on me. That is why I'm here."

The Pharisee might reply, "Really? That is why I am here too!"

The tax collector would marvel, "Wait a minute! You're religious. You're spiritual. You're a Pharisee. You've never done any of the things that I've done. You're not the person that I am."

The Pharisee would reply, "Yeah, but that is my problem. I am proud, arrogant, judgmental, and self-righteous, and I need the mercy of God. Let's make a deal: you don't think you're not good enough for God and I won't think I'm too good for God. Let's pray for each other."

This Week's Prayer: *Lord, I confess that I am a sinner in need of grace. Forgive me for thinking I'm a bit better than the next guy, and help me to see clearly.*

This Week's Question: Are you more likely to think you're too good for God or not good enough? What does Jesus say?

28

The Grace Giver

This week's Scriptures:

- Luke 15:11-32
- Psalm 103:1-14
- Psalm 78:32-39
- Isaiah 57:14-16
- Lamentations 3:19-24

A Modern Parable

In a small suburban town lived a man with a successful hardware store. His two sons worked there—the older one served as the back office accountant, while the younger managed the place. One day, the younger son told his father that he wanted out.

The father was confused and reluctant, but he walked him back to the office, opened the safe, and handed him half the money that was stored inside. The son stuffed the cash in his bag and was gone, to crash with a friend and spend his dad's money on food, drink, and drugs.

When money ran low, he eventually sold his grandfather's old car that his dad had given him after he graduated. Before he knew it, he was living on the street, earning cash selling goods he had stolen from local stores. Hungry, desperate, spirit broken, he finally decided to return home.

Even the part-timers at my dad's store have more than I do, he thought. *I'll beg him to let me stock the shelves.*

He thumbed a ride back home and walked in the front door of the store. When his dad saw him, he bolted through the store, knocking over a display, and wrapped his son in his arms, weeping. The store was full of customers, but the father didn't care if he made a fool of himself. He was just happy the son was home.

Looking on, the older brother, ticked off that his dad received his wayward son, couldn't wrap his mind around his dad's reaction.

Two Groups

You may recognize this retelling of the "Parable of the Prodigal Son," although that's not a good name for it. Not even Jesus called it that. He begins the story in Luke 15:11, "There was a man who had *two* sons." There are two brothers, and they represent every person in this world who is separated from God.

Two groups of people had come to listen to Jesus that day, and each one is represented by one of the two sons. There were the bad guys: the tax collectors and sinners. Then you have the good guys: the Pharisees. They were the churchgoers. They were the fundamentalists. They were full of judgment and empty of mercy.

One group was so bad they didn't think God would ever accept them. The other group was so good they thought God had already accepted them. Both groups were wrong.

Jesus tells a parable to show how God sees both groups. We always tend to focus on the son who comes back home, but Jesus's focus is on the father. The father and his relationships are the central teaching of this parable. What we discover about him is that the Father's door is always open and the Father's message is always "welcome."

The Father Loves Us When We Rebel Against Him

The story begins with a son who evidently had everything in life you could ever want. But somehow, the root of ingratitude had bloomed into the fruit of rebellion.

The Jewish law was clear. In this case, the older son would get two-thirds of the inheritance and the younger son would get one-third. There was only one catch: the father needed to be dead.

It was as if the younger son was saying to his father, "I wish you were dead."

If you're a parent, can you imagine hearing anything more devastating from your children? This son has dishonored, disgraced, and disowned his father.

A typical father in that day would have slapped his son across the face, kicked him out of the house, and disowned him in front of the entire community. But not only does this father ignore the insult, he does the unthinkable by granting his son's request.

At first everything goes as planned for this boy. He bought the beachfront condo, drove the Ferrari, had a Rolex on his wrist, and a different woman in his bed every night.

Then, he blew it. He lost it all. This boy lost everything *except* his father's love.

Every one—no matter who you are, where you are, or what you've done—has a Father who loves them. There is no limit to how far he will let you go, but there is also no limit to how long he will wait for you to return.

The Father Accepts Us When We Return to Him

The poet Robert Frost famously said, "Home is the place where, when you have to go there, they have to take you in."

Just like a pigeon, the homing instinct had kicked in on this kid and he wanted to go home. There is one door that is always open, and that is the door to the Father's house.

The son, who had strutted out the front door, is now slinking up the dirt road as his father is setting a record for the hundred-yard dash to get to his boy. Ancient Hebrew culture considered running to be an undignified act for an older man. Men wore long flowing robes and tunics, and they would have to gather all these up around their waist to run and would expose their undergarments. But love doesn't care what other people think.

This is how our heavenly Father treats everybody who decides to come home. He sees us with the eyes of forgiveness.

The Father Pursues Us When We Reject Him

The older son is so angry he takes the radical step of breaking his relationship with his father. For a son to refuse to go to any party or banquet a father hosted was an unspeakable public insult.

Neither son wanted to be at this party. The younger son was embarrassed, because he didn't think he deserved the party. The older son was angry, because he thought *he* deserved it. The real problem with the older brother, though, was that he compared himself to someone he'd deemed unrighteous.

Do you know why a lot of younger brothers are still out there in the pigpen and don't want to come into the church? They see a church full of older brothers who don't want them to come and are afraid if they do come, they will be slapped with the cold hand of judgment rather than touched with the warm hand of love.

Self-righteous people think that unrighteous people can never be forgiven and should never be forgiven. But while the older brother is into punishment, the father is into pardon. The older brother is into guilt, but the father is into grace. The older brother is into revenge, but the father is into reconciliation.

No matter how far you've wandered, no matter how low you've sunk, know that upon your return, you will find the Father in front of an open door with open arms and a loving heart.

This Week's Prayer: *Lord, make me an agent of your grace by teaching me to stand with arms open wide to welcome your child who has wandered.*

This Week's Question: What are the ways in which you, like the older brother, have refused to extend the grace you've received?

29

Discerner of the Heart

This week's Scriptures:

- Matthew 13:24-30
- 2 Corinthians 11:12-15
- Galatians 1:6-9
- 1 John 2:3-11
- 1 John 2:18-23

Treasure from Trash

The Italian violin maker, Antonio Stradivari, was a poor man. And yet his violins are now the most-prized violins ever made because of the rich and resonant sound they produce. The unique sound of a Stradivarius cannot be duplicated.

What may surprise you is that these precious instruments were not made from treasured pieces of wood; they were carved from discarded lumber. Because Stradivari couldn't afford fine materials, he got most of his wood from the dirty harbors where he lived. He would take those waterlogged pieces of wood to his shop, clean them up, and dry them out. Then, from those trashed pieces of lumber, he would create instruments of rare beauty.

It has since been discovered that while the wood floated in those dirty harbors, microbes infiltrated the wood and ate out the centers of those cells. This left just a fibrous infrastructure of wood that created resonating chambers for the music. From wood that nobody wanted, Stradivari produced violins that now everybody wants.[7] Just as this poor violin maker transformed trash into treasure, only God can transform you into what you were truly meant to be.

Only God Can Tell Sinners from Saints

When Jesus was teaching, the greatest threat to any farmer was that someone might, because of anger or hostility, sow *weeds* in his field of wheat. If you sowed weeds in a neighbor's wheat field, you ruined the entire crop and took away his only source of income. This was such a serious crime that Rome established a law prohibiting it. And, unfortunately, you cannot tell the difference between wheat and tares until they both ripen together. The counterfeit looks just like the original.

Jesus says that this can be true of his Father's kingdom:

> "The kingdom of heaven may be compared to a man who sowed good seed in his field, but while his men were sleeping, his enemy came and sowed weeds among the wheat and went away. So when the plants came up and bore grain, then the weeds appeared also" (Matthew 13:24-26).

Jesus identifies the one who sows the bad seed, the enemy, as the devil (Matthew 13:39). Satan is not an innovator; he is an imitator. His counterfeits are people. While God is sowing the good seeds of his saints, Satan is sowing the bad seeds of his sinners.

Appearance of Righteousness

In 2 Corinthians 11, Paul reveals exactly how the master counterfeiter works. First, he offers a counterfeit *savior*: "For even Satan disguises himself as an angel of light" (2 Corinthians 11:14). So while there are cults that preach Jesus, it is not the Christ of Christianity that they preach.

Satan also offers counterfeit *servants*: "For such men are false apostles, deceitful workmen, disguising themselves as apostles of Christ…So it is no surprise if his servants, also, disguise themselves as servants of righteousness. Their end will correspond to their deeds" (2 Corinthians 11:13,15).

The third thing the enemy produces is counterfeit *saints*. Paul identifies these "false brethren" as people who appear to be your brother on the outside, but are your enemy on the inside (Galatians 2:4).

Galatians 1:8 even asserts that the deceiver offers a counterfeit *salvation*: "But even if we, or an angel from heaven, preach any other gospel to you than what we have preached to you, let him be accursed." It is not that Christians masquerade as children of the devil, but rather that the ungodly often appear to be righteous.

God can tell a sinner from a saint. You're going to find both inside the church just as you will outside it. Jesus never pretended that the church was perfect, and we shouldn't either. In every church there are people who claim to be Christians but don't act like Christians.

Only God Can Take Sinners from Saints

Taking the weeds out of the wheat field is not our job. We must focus on cultivating wheat, and then let God do the dividing. Why?

First, the plant roots of both the good and the bad would have become closely intertwined, and even if you could distinguish between the two, you would wind up uprooting wheat as well as weeds.

But also wheat that was planted or germinated later would mature later, and some of the wheat that had not yet produced heads of grain would be mistaken for weeds. *The dividing could not take place until the harvest was ripe.*

I'll be honest. The church has, at times, been guilty of sin—even to the point of shedding blood—by trying to remove the weeds from the wheat. During the crusades of the Middle Ages, unbelievable brutality was committed against non-Christians, especially Muslims and Jews, in the name of Jesus. During the Inquisition, countless thousands of Christians, who would not submit to the dogma and authority of the Catholic Church, were imprisoned, tortured, and executed.

That's why Christians should be the greatest defenders of religious freedom in the world. We are to be people of compassion, not people of coercion.

It's God's job to take the sinners from the saints.

When the Reaper Reaps

You may be wondering how the Reaper knows the wheat from the weeds. What distinguishes them is the spiritual fruit they bear. Weeds may be *similar* to wheat, but weeds cannot produce wheat kernels. The mature grain will always set the wheat apart from the weeds.

Are you a weed or are you wheat?

Whether you are a Baptist or a Catholic, baptized or not, religious or nonreligious, a church member or not, is all irrelevant. The question that matters is: Are you a weed or are you wheat? And the answer can be gleaned from one other question: Who is your Father? That alone will determine where you spend eternity.

For two thousand years the Lord has been sowing generation after generation of his saints into the world. They are scattered everywhere. They take root, flourish, bear fruit, and give witness to the fact that God is at work all over the world.

Yet, in a spiritual sense, all wheat stalks begin as weeds. There was a time when you and I were not wheat; we were weeds. There was a time when you and I were not saints; we were sinners. We needed a Savior who could turn us into saints.

Turning a sinner into a saint is something only God can do.

This Week's Prayer: *Lord, I confess that it is not my job to judge between weeds and wheat; it is yours. I long to be fruitful for your kingdom.*

This Week's Question: As one who was once a weed, how is Jesus using you to draw others into fruitful relationship with him?

30

A Divine Divider

This week's Scriptures:

- Luke 16:19-31
- Matthew 25:31-46
- Revelation 20:11-15
- Matthew 7:21-23
- 2 Thessalonians 1:5-10

Eternal Reversal

A well-to-do man and his family lived in a plush, gated neighborhood in a wealthy community. By all accounts, he was a righteous man.

"I've never met a better man than that one," someone remarked at church. "He's sure blessed."

At night, when the man turned into his neighborhood, he would always catch a glimpse of a young lady on the far street corner wearing tattered clothes. He never stopped to help her—not because he assumed she'd use his money on cheap vodka or heroine. After all, he reasoned, she could get a job if she wanted one.

Years later, the man and the girl died the same hour, he from an auto collision and she from exposure to the cold. She went to the presence of God and he to eternal torment.

When the man recognized the apostle Paul on the border between heaven and hell, he cried out for mercy.

"I'm sorry," Paul replied. "You already had heaven on earth while the woman you ignored lived in hell."

"Then I beg you, Paul, send her back to tell my family. Let her warn them."

"But they hear the Gospel preached every Sunday," Paul replied.

"They know of the commands to care for the poor, the exhortations to selflessness, the story of the Good Samaritan."

"But it will be more powerful if they hear from someone who has come back from the dead."

"They already have," Paul replied.

Our Final Exit

I asked my ninety-three-year-old mother the other day if she feared dying. She gave me an answer I hear so often: "I don't fear dying in and of itself. It's just the unknown. You only do it once, so you don't get to practice."

Jesus told the story of the rich man and Lazarus to clear up *some* of that unknown (Luke 16). The two men in the story were different in so many ways. They were different in their *positions*. In the eyes of society, one was a somebody and the other was a nobody. They were different in their *possessions*. One was a billionaire and the other was a beggar. They were different in their *passions*. One loved gold and the other loved God. These differences determined their divergent destinies.

Nobody gets to determine how they enter this world. You didn't get to determine the place of your birth, the time of your birth, or even the color of your skin. What we do get to determine is how we *leave* this world. You didn't get to determine your entrance. You do get to determine your exit.

But you don't make that decision at the moment you breathe your final breath. Rather, *today's decision determines tomorrow's destiny*.

Live Right

The first man is rich. The verb tense used here indicates that this rich man dressed himself every day in purple. He had other clothes, but purple cloth was the most expensive cloth you could buy and only the wealthiest people could afford it. In other words, this man dressed in a $3000 tailored suit every day. He was a clotheshorse. He wanted everybody to know he had money and plenty of it.

Then Jesus introduces poor Lazarus. He couldn't walk. His body was covered with sores. He was hungry, emaciated, sick, and in every way the complete opposite of the man on the other side of the gate.

But the *major* difference between these two men was not that one was rich and the other man was poor. A quick read of the story would give you the impression that one man was condemned because he was rich, and the other was commended because he was poor. And yet God doesn't put a premium on poverty, nor does he put a penalty on prosperity. It's not a vice to be rich and it's not a virtue to be poor.

What differentiated these two men was not what they owned but what owned them.

The poor man has something the rich man doesn't: a *name*. This is the only story that Jesus ever tells where one of the players has a name. He gives this man a name because his name is important.

The name "Lazarus" means, "the one God helps" or "in God I trust." Lazarus had a relationship with God.

Look Ahead

When the two men die, everything is suddenly reversed. Lazarus, who had nothing but God, now has everything. The rich man, who had everything but God, now has nothing. Lazarus's body wasn't even given a decent burial. Back in that day, poor people were thrown into a garbage dump called Gehenna and their bodies were burned. Rich people would be buried in the finest tomb available, anointed with the most expensive perfumes, and wrapped in the most expensive cloth.

Lazarus died and was carried by the angels to Abraham's side. Jewish listeners will understand that to mean "paradise." The custom in that day was to seat the most honored and respected guests next to the host. The most honored place a Jew could have would be the side of Abraham, the father of the Jewish race. Poor Lazarus didn't have much of a funeral, but he had some unbelievable pallbearers!

People are not ready to meet God because they are so spiritually near-sighted. They can see only as far as today, but they're not looking ahead to tomorrow. Yet *today's decision determines tomorrow's destiny.*

Listen to God

We are told specifically that Lazarus was "comforted." No more hunger: he is dining at God's table. No more sickness: he is permanently healed. No more poverty: he is walking golden streets surrounded by pearly gates. No more homelessness: he is living in a room custom built by the master carpenter. No more loneliness: he is now living permanently with a friend who sticks closer than a brother.

The rich man? That is another story. We are told that this man is tortured and tormented.

A teacher was telling a story about the rich man and Lazarus from a children's Bible. He pointed out how one man was rich and one man was poor while they were on this earth. After they died, he pointed out how one man went to be with God and one man went to live without God. After he got through with the lesson, he said, "Now boys, who would you rather be? The rich man or Lazarus?" One quick-thinking kid raised his hand and said, "I'd like to be the rich man while I'm alive and Lazarus when I'm dead."

That is what we all wish, but it doesn't work that way. Today's decision determines tomorrow's destiny. Begin now to live for God, look to God, and listen to God for that is the only life that will matter both today and tomorrow.

This Week's Prayer: *Lord, thank you for your Word, which guides us into all truth. Quicken my heart to receive and respond to your Gospel today.*

This Week's Question: Where are you in this parable? Do you know God intimately, like Lazarus, or is this a wake-up call for you?

Jesus, the Teacher

Scholars debate almost everything about who Jesus was and what he did. But all agree he was a masterful teacher. He spoke with an understanding of spirituality and philosophical depth that continues to dazzle the minds of the masses. His teaching addresses life's most pressing problems and helps us navigate through them. The trick is to encounter Jesus's familiar phrases and well-trod wisdom with fresh eyes.

31

Flying Standby

This week's Scriptures:

- Matthew 7:1-6
- 1 Corinthians 2:14-16
- John 12:44-50
- Romans 2:1-11
- Romans 14:1-12

First Impressions

Two young men walk into church. They both are the same age, twenty-two. Same height, same weight, and same build.

The first young man, clean-cut and fresh-shaven, walks in wearing a crisply starched long-sleeved polo shirt, freshly ironed slacks, and wearing shoes in the latest style. The second walks in wearing a T-shirt, blue jeans with more holes than pockets, flip-flops, tattoos on both arms, a nose ring, and orange hair.

Immediately, if we are honest, most of us would look at the first guy and think, *He needs to meet my daughter (or my sister)*. And we'd look at the second and think, *He needs to meet Jesus*.

I forgot to tell you the first man is an atheist, has a live-in girlfriend, and is addicted to pornography. The second is passionately committed to Jesus Christ, lives a life of purity, and wants to be a missionary.

In a book called *UnChristian*, David Kinnaman describes why the church is failing to reach the next generation. When nineteen- to twenty-five-year-olds were asked to give their perception of Christianity, the top three things they listed were: antihomosexual, judgmental, and hypocritical. And studies show that almost 60 percent of Americans between the ages of eighteen and twenty-five have significantly altered their appearance at some point in their lives using tattoos, dying their hair an untraditional color, or piercing their body in a place other than an earlobe.[8]

Rather than feeling welcomed, young people have felt judged by the church.

To Judge or Not to Judge

If we're honest, we've all sat in the seat of the judge, and we've sat in the seat of the judged.

Perhaps at one point in your life you left church because of an overbearing judgmentalist. If that's the case, I am sorry. With that said, it's critical to understand what the Bible says and doesn't say about being judgmental.

Everyone knows that God gave Moses the Ten Commandments. There was a time when you could put those commandments up in courthouses and schools all over this country. But we are living in an age when many have added an eleventh commandment. You won't notice it hanging on walls, but it's trumpeted in office buildings, college classrooms, schools, and country clubs all over this country. Our favorite commandment has become, *You shall not judge.*

This admonition, spoken by Jesus in Matthew 7:1, is probably the most misunderstood, misused, and misapplied verse in the entire Bible. I call it the "world's favorite Scripture." Unfortunately, most people don't understand what Jesus meant. That's why he continues on to explain his meaning. What he says may surprise you, because if you were to ask Jesus, "Should we judge or not?" his answer would be, "It all depends." There is a way we can judge without being judgmental.

Eliminate Improper Judgment

The word Jesus uses for "judge" is the Greek word *krino,* which means "to discriminate" or "to make a difference." Here it means to offer a criticism that is either unfair or unjustified. Because it was spoken in the Sermon on the Mount, these words were directed to Jesus's disciples. What he was saying was, "You ought to be the least judgmental of people and yet you battle being the most judgmental."

Too often we get more concerned about the outside of a person than we do about the inside of a person. If we don't like tattoos, we judge people who wear them. If we don't drink, we judge people who do. If we wear certain types of clothes to church, we judge people who don't. It has been rightly said, "Never mistake the moment for the man." Don't make snap judgments, and don't judge just by a first impression or just by appearance.

It's important to note that there is a difference between confronting a sin and condemning a sinner. Not all judgment is wrong. One helpful rule of thumb—to discern that fine line between confronting a sin and condemning the sinner—is that God's Word is a reliable guide. If you use another standard, you're being judgmental. Yet it is never wrong to call wrong *wrong* when God calls it wrong.

Participate in Self-Judgment

Jesus presses further by asking his disciples, "Why do you see the speck that is in your brother's eye, but do not notice the log that is in your own eye?" (Matthew 7:3).

If you'd been in Jesus's audience, you would have been laughing your head off. The picture painted here is just hilarious. Here is a man staring down a splinter in one man's eye while he has a two-by-four sticking out of his own. Do you know what a splinter is? Just a piece of a log. Jesus said we are criticizing a fault we have in our own life. We tend to see a splinter in someone else's eye as a log, while we see a log in our eye as just a splinter.

If you want to see what you look like, you look in a mirror. If you want to see what someone else looks like, you look out a window. Jesus is saying we need to spend more time looking in the mirror and less time looking out the window. The next time you see a splinter in someone else's life, look for the log that is in your own. Remember, the splinter is just a piece of the log. What you see in others is just a reflection of what you see in you.

Validate Righteous Judgment

Jesus uses the word *hypocrite* (Matthew 7:5)—one of the three things young people today thought about when they heard the word *Christian*.

A hypocrite is someone who looks out the window but never looks in the mirror. Jesus never said, "You are wrong to look out the window." What he is saying is, "Always first look in the mirror." Most people misunderstand what Jesus said because they try to make Jesus say something he *didn't* say and they don't hear him saying something that he *did* say.

What Jesus was saying was that as we encounter someone in need of correction, we should first look for the log and then deal with the splinter. First look in the mirror, and then look out the window. Jesus is not forbidding judgment that is done at the right time, in the right place, in the right way, with the right spirit. One of the marks of a spiritual person is someone who knows how to judge correctly. First Corinthians 2:15 says, "The spiritual person judges all things." It is not wrong to confront a person who has sin in their life.

God's judgment is meant to draw us closer to him. Jesus died on the cross and was raised from the dead so that we could escape ultimate judgment. Come to the One who doesn't want to be your judge, but wants to be your Lord and your Savior.

This Week's Prayer: *Lord, teach me to see myself and others clearly, so that I might be more aware of my own sin and more passionate about your grace for sinners like me.*

This Week's Question: What is the "log" that you most often see in others? Does it suggest what your own "splinter" is?

32

A Prayer Warrior

This week's Scriptures:

- Matthew 6:5-8
- Romans 8:26-30
- James 5:13-18
- Psalm 141:1-2
- Psalm 4:1-5

Hear Me Now?

If you're anything like me, you have, cell phone in hand and blood pressure rising, uttered these frustrating words: "Can you hear me now?"

Do you ever feel that way about prayer? Do you ever worry, "Can he hear me now?" Do you ever wonder if—like phone calls—your prayers ever get dropped?

Prayer is the biggest struggle I have in my Christian life. It's difficult to maintain a consistent prayer life, and especially difficult to sustain the conviction that it does any good at times.

Do you ever feel that way?

Prayer doesn't come naturally for most people. Often intercession feels as much like a *battle* as a *blessing*. I know that prayer is supposed to be a dialogue, but it often feels like a monologue. There is nothing worse than trying to carry on a conversation with someone who won't talk back.

We are all looking for the code breaker, the way to crack God's safe. People don't like to put it this crudely, but here is what we are really asking about prayer:

"How can I pray so that God will give me what I want?"

Graciously, even when we ask the wrong question, God is still willing to give us the right answer.

Lesson Worth Learning

A PhD student at Princeton University once went into the office of Albert Einstein and asked, "What is there left in the world for original dissertation research?"

The brilliant scientist replied, "Find out about prayer. Somebody must find out about prayer."[9]

Einstein wasn't the only one with a curiosity about prayer. Jesus taught on it, too, and he did so because the disciples *asked* him to. They may not have been interested in producing dissertations on prayer, but they wanted to know *how* to pray. It's the only time in the Bible where one person explicitly teaches another person how to pray. This all came out of a request from the disciples.

> Now Jesus was praying in a certain place, and when he finished, one of his disciples said to him, "Lord, teach us to pray, as John taught his disciples" (Luke 11:1).

The disciples had been watching Jesus pray. They had been listening to Jesus pray. Evidently the way he prayed was so different from the way that they prayed that they said, "We are not doing this right. Something is not working."

They went to Jesus and said, "Show us how to do what you do. Show us how to pray the way that you pray."

Pray Secretly

Amazingly, the first thing that Jesus talks about is not *how* to pray but *where* to pray (Matthew 6:5-6). I know that may sound strange to you, because we all know you can pray anywhere. You may pray doing your makeup while traveling down the freeway talking on your cell phone!

The first advice Jesus gives on prayer is to do it in private.

In the first century the Pharisees—ultraconservative, fundamentalist legalists who saw God in terms of rules, regulations, and religion—loved to pray in two places: in the synagogue and on the street corner.

And their timing was impeccable. Every afternoon sacrifices would be offered at the temple. At the same time, every day a trumpet would blow and would signal that it was time to pray. Wherever you were and whatever you were doing, you were expected to stop and pray. The Pharisees, who loved to show just how pious they were, realized this was a great time to showcase their spirituality, babbling loudly enough for everybody to hear.

Jesus wasn't condemning public praying. The Bible is full of public prayer, and most prayers recorded in the Bible were offered before other people. The point that Jesus was making was don't pray for show. Prayer is not to impress people; prayer is to interact with God.

Pray Sincerely

Jesus said that real prayer, attention-getting prayer, God-honoring prayer, heaven-satisfying prayer is not just prayed secretly but prayed *sincerely*.

Jesus adds that your Father rewards what is done in secret. He's saying *secrecy fosters sincerity*. God knows that when you take the time to go to a secret place and get alone with him, you are sincere about what you are doing. When you are in that secret place, there is no applause and nobody is clapping for your religious performance, for how skillful you are in talking to God.

If you have something extremely sensitive and important to talk to someone about, you may offer, "We need to find a place where we can talk." You want to make sure that you are heard and you want to make sure that you hear. When you shut out the noise of this world, you maximize your ability to hear God. It shows God that you are taking your relationship with utmost seriousness.

Do you have that secret place? Do you have that place designated where you can be alone with God?

It can be anywhere. It can be your closet, your basement, your spare bedroom, but you need to have a place of rendezvous where you go and show you mean business with God.

Pray Specifically

Jesus goes a step further in telling us what *not* to pray.

"And when you pray, do not heap up empty phrases as the Gentiles do, for they think that they will be heard for their many words" (Matthew 6:7).

Now the word for "heard" means "to be taken seriously." In other words, God is not moved by the quantity of your words.

You could pretty much sum up most prayers like this: "God, thank you for your blessings. Please continue to bless me. If you will continue to bless me, I'll continue to thank you for your blessings. Amen."

But Jesus makes the point that it is not how much you say to God that causes him to hear your prayer, but it is how you say what you say that gets his attention.

"Do not be like them, for your Father knows what you need before you ask him" (Matthew 6:8).

Prayer is not primarily about telling God what you need or want. It is for the purpose of getting closer to and going deeper with God.

It's almost as if God is saying, "Don't bring me your shopping list. I already know what is on it. We will deal with that later. Bring me your heart. Bring me your love. Bring me your undivided attention. Bring me your undiluted affection."

In other words, prayer is not primarily about getting things *from* God; it's about spending time *with* God.

This Week's Prayer: *Lord, ignite my passion to grow in intimacy with you. This week I bring you my heart. I bring you my love. I bring you my undivided attention.*

This Week's Question: Where is the physical space where you can share secrets with God?

33

Focused on the Father

This week's Scriptures:

- Matthew 6:9-10
- Ephesians 5:15-20
- James 4:13-17
- Romans 15:8-15
- Hebrews 10:32-39

How You Should Pray

When brand-new subdivisions are under construction, they often feature a model home that you can walk through to get an idea of the kind of home you'll have if you buy in that neighborhood. If you want to know what a home from that builder looks like and feels like and would be like to live in, you can go into one of these model homes.

The prayer that Jesus teaches his disciples is a *model* prayer. His posse had overheard him praying on countless occasions and asked him to teach them how to pray. And he did what they asked! Jesus said if you want to pray in such a way that you know your prayer will be effective and that God will hear you, this is the way to do it. Jesus did not say this is "*what* you should pray." He said this is "*how* you should pray."

This passage, found in Matthew 6:9-15 and commonly known as the Lord's Prayer, is not a spell or magic formula. Jesus is not saying that these words that you can mindlessly recite are all there is to prayer. This prayer is a pattern that lays down some principles that will teach us how to pray. It is not a mechanical prayer but a model prayer.

Focus on the Father's Worship

The first two words would have stunned the crowd that listened to Jesus that day. There is no evidence of anyone, before Jesus Christ, ever using the term *Father* to address God. Yahweh is referred to as "Father" fourteen times, but always in relation to the nation of Israel. Never to an individual. But Jesus called God "Father" more than sixty times in his own prayers. The expression that Jesus often used was the Aramaic word *Abba*, which means "Papa" or "Daddy." If you are a child of God, you can spiritually crawl up into his lap, put your arms around his neck, call him "Daddy," and talk to him just like a child talks to a father.

He is not just a personal Father but a *powerful* Father. Verse 9 goes on to say he is our Father "in heaven." Perhaps you wonder, "Where is God when bad things happen to good people? Where is God when you watch the waves of injustice roll over the shores of our courtrooms? Where is God when innocent babies die and guilty criminals go free?" The answer is, he is in heaven and nothing escapes his notice.

Jesus adds "hallowed be your name" (Matthew 6:9). To hallow God's name means "to honor it," to make sure it gets the respect that it deserves. I often ask myself, *Will the prayer that I am about to pray honor God's name?*

Focus on the Father's Will

Then Jesus prays, "Your kingdom come, your will be done, on earth as it is in heaven" (Matthew 6:10).

The kingdom is a place where a king rules and reigns. When you ask God's kingdom to come, you are asking God to sit on the throne of your heart and your life so that his will will be done in both.

This is the hardest part of this prayer. The number one priority of prayer is not to get God to do what you want, but to get God to do what he wants.

That is why this part of the prayer is difficult. Before you ask for anything, before you tell him what you want, before you tell him what you need, say right up front, "I am taking my plans, my ambitions, my goals, my agendas, my desires, and I am surrendering them all to you."

You can't move forward with God in any prayer until you get this issue settled. Before you get to your wants, your desires, your agenda, you have to go to God and say, "I want your will to be done."

The Best Prayer You Can Pray

Seeking God's will above our own isn't easy.

It wasn't even easy for Jesus!

Did you know the only time Scripture records Jesus wrestling in prayer was in the Garden of Gethsemane? What was his struggle? He wrestled over the will of God, and he could not go to the cross until he finally said to God, "Not my will, but yours be done."

The trouble comes in our lives when we don't pray this part of the prayer. The trouble comes when we focus on our will and not his. That is when marriages fall apart. That is when business decisions go bad. That is when you experience the kind of moral failure that can scar you with unbelievable guilt.

The best prayer you can ever pray for anyone, in any situation, at any time, in any place, is the prayer, "Your will be done." Do you know why? Because God's will is always the right and best thing to pray for.

The purpose of prayer isn't about getting your will done in heaven; it's about seeing *his* will done in your heart. It is not to get God in line with your desires but to help you line up with his.

Prayer Changes Things

When you surrender your will to his will, you find that prayer changes you. Your prayers will change as well. That is why getting into that secret place every day and surrendering your will to his is so important. Don't ever leave the place of prayer until you are fully surrendered to Jesus Christ. Without surrender, nothing will change in your life. Nothing will change the perspective of your life. Nothing will change the purpose of your life. Nothing will change the priority of your life like completely being surrendered to his will.

When we pray, we want to know that God hears us. God says, "First, I want your worship. Focus on who I am, where I live, and what I want, because then you will want my will." You will never experience the power and joy of prayer until you are willing to find and do his will.

I encourage you, perhaps over the next month, to take the first five minutes of each day and give God your worship. Focus on who he is, where he lives, and what he wants. Surrender to his will and watch how God changes your life.

This Week's Prayer: *Lord, quiet the voices in my heart that are all about* me. *Tip my face toward yours so that I might greet you with worship, acknowledging who* you *are.*

This Week's Question: As you shift your gaze toward God, how is he inviting you to do his will on earth?

34

The One Who Provides

Learning to Pray

According to the latest Gallup poll, more Americans will pray this week than will exercise, drive a car, have sex, or go to work. Some 90 percent of us pray regularly and 75 percent of us pray every day.[10]

Every faith and every religion have some form of prayer. Throughout history even the most remote tribes have been found to present offerings and pray to their gods for the same things that we pray for. The ancient Incas and Aztecs even sacrificed humans trying to attract the gods' attention. Devout Muslims stop whatever they are doing to pray five times a day. Buddhists have their prayer wheels. Millions in AA groups pray daily to a higher power, begging for help in overcoming their addiction. Philip Yancey writes, "We pray because we just can't help but pray."[11]

We pray because we have problems that only God can solve, questions that only God can answer, and needs that only God can meet. That is why we do need to learn how to open up to God in our prayer life.

And as we learn *from Jesus* how to pray, we have the confidence that God *hears* our prayers. He hears me as I pray for you, and he hears you as you pray for me.

Ask God to Provide Your Needs

As we continue unpacking the prayer Jesus teaches his disciples, there is a shift in emphasis in the first two words of Matthew 6:11, "Give us." The first part of the prayer focuses on God and his nature. Now the focus shifts to us and our needs.

When I was a boy, Christmas took on a whole new meaning when I was finally able to earn my own money to buy presents. Until then, my mom and dad had given me money to buy them their Christmas gifts. And I did, as a child, what adults too often do with much of what God gives us: instead of using it to bless *them,* I used it to bless *me*! I bought each parent a long string of bubblegum balls and a Milky Way candy bar because I knew they would wind up giving it back to me. (Against my protest, my dad ate the Milky Way!)

For many of us who like to *receive,* our favorite word in the Lord's Prayer is *give.*

But, you may protest, it was Jesus's word. Indeed, there's a method to his madness, because whenever you ask someone for a gift, you acknowledge:

1. They own it.
2. You need it.
3. They don't owe it to you.
4. You don't deserve it.

The words "give us" remind us what our relationship to God is actually like: we are completely dependent on him and he is completely independent of us.

What to Ask For?

So, what's worth asking for?

Jesus says *bread* is worth asking for.

In the Hebrew mind, bread was indispensable to sustaining life. Bread was considered so sacred in the Middle East that it was broken when served, not sliced. That is where we get the expression "breaking bread." Here, bread represents all that we need to meet our needs.

Jesus was teaching us that it's not wrong to ask God to meet the needs we have in our lives.

This prayer has nothing to do with our wants. We're asking God for bread, not pie. God has promised to meet our needs; he has not promised to meet our greeds. We may want cake, but what we may need is bread. Jesus's prayer teaches us that God meets our needs one day at a time. God doesn't provide for today's needs tomorrow. He is never late. God does not provide for tomorrow's needs today. He is never early.

Whether we have a little bread or a loaf of bread, these few words teach us to be *thankful*. We're encouraged to remember where all good gifts come from. As the apostle Paul told a pagan crowd in Athens, "[God] himself gives everyone life and breath and everything else" (Acts 17:25 NIV).

Ask God to Pardon Your Sins

Only two things can come between you and God.

One is unconfessed sin. The psalmist says, "If I regard wickedness in my heart, the Lord will not hear" (Psalm 66:18 NASB). So we are to pray, "Forgive us our debts." The word *forgive* means "to cancel a debt." Sin is a debt. We exist to worship and obey God. When we don't, we owe a sin-debt to God.

The only remedy for this debt is to declare spiritual bankruptcy, to go into a spiritual Chapter 11 and let somebody else pay the debt. That is exactly what Jesus Christ did on the cross. When Jesus Christ died on the cross and paid for our sins, he gave us the ability and the right to go to God and say, "Forgive us our debts."

Besides unforgiven sin, the other thing that can come between you and God is an unforgiving spirit. So we continue to pray, "as we also have forgiven our debtors" (Matthew 6:12).

When you pray these words, you are asking God to forgive you *in the same way you forgive others*. It's a dangerous prayer to pray! If you're not willing to forgive the debts of others, you are actually asking God not to forgive you. That is not a prayer you want God to answer.

Ask God to Protect Your Purity

When Jesus teaches us to pray, it may sound like a strange request that we not be led into temptation and that we be delivered from evil. A holy God obviously would never lead his people into a situation where they would become unholy! James 1:13 says, "Let no one say when he is tempted, 'I am being tempted by God,' for God cannot be tempted with evil, and he himself tempts no one."

You could paraphrase Jesus's prayer this way: "Lord, don't allow me to walk into a situation that would overwhelm me and cause me to sin, but deliver me from temptation and from the devil and every trap that he would set for me."

There is a reason "do not lead us into temptation" follows "forgive us our sins." How many times have you had to go to God and confess the same sin over and over and over and over? I believe if we spent more time asking God to deliver us from temptation, we would spend less time asking God to forgive us our sins.

We have to go to God, acknowledge our needs, and ask God to meet those needs. When you pray, you let God do the fighting. Prayer is not just for defense. Prayer is for offense.

This Week's Prayer: *Lord, don't allow me to walk into a situation that would cause me to sin; deliver me from the devil and every trap that he would set for me.*

This Week's Question: What do you *need* this day? Are you trusting that God provides for your needs one day at a time?

35

The Treasure Principle

This week's Scriptures:

- Matthew 6:19-24
- Mark 10:23-27
- Luke 18:18-26
- 1 Timothy 6:17-19
- Luke 6:38

Final Plans

I'd been putting it off for a good while. Mainly, I just didn't want to deal with it. Recently, Teresa and I finally took the plunge. I thought it would be kind of miserable, but it was a ministry instead. When the results of our efforts arrived in the mail, I opened up the package and read the words on the front page: "Last Will and Testament."

The concept of the will dates back almost five thousand years. In the past, the word *will* was used to specify real estate a person was leaving to others while *testament* was used to identify the personal belongings that person wished to leave to loved ones and friends. Today, the word *will* refers to anything that is left behind.

We call it the "Last Will and Testament" because we are not going to last. One day we will have eaten our last meal, read our last book, had our last kiss, and spoken our last word. So we survey all that is ours and decide what to do with it. Yet when we take stock of everything that we call "mine," we will discover, if we haven't already, that nothing is *really* ours.

Master or Be Mastered

The Bible talks about money more than eight hundred times. And it often surprises people to learn that 15 percent of everything Jesus said related directly to money and finances. Jesus talked more about money than he talked about heaven and hell combined. Why? Because you cannot divorce your faith and your finances.

One of two things is going to happen to everything that you think you own today, everything that you think is your stuff: you are either going to lose it while you are alive or you are going to leave it once you are dead. That is why Jesus taught what I call the "Treasure Principle," found in Matthew 6:19-24.

The Treasure Principle is not so much about *giving* your money as *managing* it. There is far more in the Bible about managing your money than giving your money. The Treasure Principle comes directly from the lips of Jesus and is probably the most brilliant financial advice you will ever be given: *you cannot manage your money until you master your money*. It's why millions—who haven't learned to manage *or* master their money—listen to Clark Howard and Dave Ramsey. Yet once you understand the Treasure Principle and how to apply it in your life, you will experience real financial freedom and a joy in your life like you never have before.

Be Strategic About Where You Put Your Wealth

When Jesus referred to treasure, his earliest audience would have understood it to refer to clothing, food, or money. Rich people wore the finest clothes, but clothes could be eaten by moths. Rich people had plenty of food mainly in the form of grain and meat, but food could be eaten by rats and worms.

And people also had wealth in the form of gold and silver, but there were no banks or vaults so you had to keep your money in your house. But houses were made of clay and mud, so a thief could easily break through the wall and steal it. What Jesus was saying was, "Be careful that you don't put your treasure in what can be ruined, rotted, or robbed." He's reminding us that what we consider our treasure is not ours at all.

A great example is leasing a car. There is a big difference between owning a car and leasing a car. If you buy a car, when the payments are complete, you own it. If you lease a car, when the lease is up, you have to turn the car back in. All we have is a "lease on life." When the lease is up, we have to turn it all back in. We don't get to keep anything. Just as the car goes back to the dealer, our life goes back to the Creator.

Be Wise in How You Perceive Your Wealth

Jesus quickly shifts from being a financial counselor to being an ophthalmologist when he calls the eye "the lamp of the body" (Matthew 6:22).

As you are reading, to transmit a page of this book's print to your brain, light waves have to pass through the cornea at the front of the eye, through the pupil, and through the lens to the retina where special cells, called rods and cones, react to light. That is how light gets in through the eye, so the eye really is the "lamp of the body."

Someone has called the eye "the window of the soul." Here the eye is pictured as a window through which light comes into the body. If a window is clean and the glass is clear, the light that comes in will properly light every part of a room. If the window is dirty or the glass is discolored, the light will be hindered and the room will be dark.

Jesus is saying that the spiritual condition of your eye is determined by how your eye sees money. Jesus is not concerned with what you have. He is concerned with how you *see* what you have, because how you see what you have will determine not only what you do with it, but also what it does to you.

Be Careful How You Position Your Wealth

Jesus closes by emphasizing that either you are a master *of* your money or you are mastered *by* your money.

If Jesus had said, "You *should not* serve both God and money," this would be a question of *advisability*. If he had said, "You *must not* serve both God and money," this would be a matter of *accountability*. Instead, Jesus said, "You *cannot* serve God and money." So this is a matter of *impossibility*.

A number of years ago, Bob Dylan wrote a song that says we're "gonna have to serve somebody." Your checkbook ledger or bank account statement will tell you something about whom you're serving. Show me where your money is going, and I'll show you where your heart is flowing.

Jesus doesn't want your money. It's already his. Jesus wants your heart. But since your heart always follows your money, he wants you to surrender your money, your wealth, your stuff to him. You will never master your money until Jesus is the master of you.

This Week's Prayer: *Lord, I confess that all that I have is yours. Release my grip on all that binds my heart, so that I might be mastered by you alone.*

This Week's Question: What does this month's credit card statement, bank statement, or checkbook ledger reveal about your heart?

36

A Marriage Counselor

This week's Scriptures:

- Matthew 19:1-6
- Genesis 2:18-25
- Ephesians 5:22-33

- Romans 7:1-3
- 1 Peter 3:1-7

A Blessed Invention

I recently came across a fascinating article titled "The Top 10 Inventions that Changed the World." For the most part, there weren't any big surprises. The list included the wheel, the printing press, the steam engine, the lightbulb, the Internet.

One that didn't make the list has, in my opinion, had more influence than any other product ever invented. This one isn't a product as much as a *relationship*. To me the world's greatest invention, established at the beginning of time, is marriage.

Where marriage has been practiced as God intended, it has brought more good, blessed more cultures, and boosted more societies than any other invention. Yet today, that invention is being tinkered with, tested, and torn apart.

Time magazine published an article not long ago titled, "Why Marriage Matters," noting the breakdown of the American family over the last forty years: "How much does [marriage] matter? More than words can say. There is no single force causing as much measureable hardship and human misery in this country as the collapse of marriage."[12]

That's one person's opinion. The opinion that matters is the opinion of the person who invented marriage. Even though Jesus was never married, he knew more about marriage than any counselor or pastor who has ever lived, because he invented it. In just a few short sentences in Matthew 19, Jesus gives an encyclopedia of truth about marriage, about divorce, and about love.

God's Default Position

The Pharisees, testing Jesus, asked him whether it could ever be lawful to divorce one's wife. In modern lingo, they were asking, "Is there any such thing as a 'no fault' divorce?" (Matthew 19:3).

California was the first state in the country to pass a law saying that you could get divorced for any reason or none at all. The legislation is now on the books in all fifty states.

In the first century, two prominent rabbis promoted two primary schools of thought about divorce. One was liberal and one was more conservative. The liberal view said that if your wife burned the biscuits, you could get a divorce. If your wife had too many wrinkles, you could get a divorce. If she looked bad or cooked bad, you could tell her, "Hit the road, Jackie!" The other school of thought was a lot more conservative and limited divorce to cases where some type of sexual sin occurred.

Yet instead of answering the question, "How can you get *out* of a marriage?" Jesus answered this question: "Why should you stay *in* a marriage?" The Pharisees had been asking the wrong question. Jesus gives the right answer to the right question—short, succinct, simple, but garlic-breath strong.

> "Have you not read that he who created them from the beginning made them male and female, and said, 'Therefore a man shall leave his father and his mother and hold fast to his wife, and the two shall become one flesh'? So they are no longer two but one flesh. What therefore God has joined together, let not man separate" (Matthew 19:4-6).

Jesus quoted Genesis 2 and said, "There's your answer." It's God's default position for marriage, available in fifty states and around the globe.

Understand God's Plan for Marriage

The "them" Jesus referred to in verse 4 is the first married couple in history: Adam and Eve. God created them male and female. From the beginning, God built several qualities into what makes a marriage a marriage.

First, God designed *duality*. It takes two to get married. That is why God created "them," not just "him." The second characteristic is *heterosexuality*. God did not create them male and male. He did not create them female and female. He created them male and female. The only picture in God's album of marriage is that of a man and a woman. The third characteristic is *monogamy*. He did not create male and females. He did not create males and female. He created male and female—one man, one woman, one life.

This is God's plan for marriage.

Remember God's Purpose for Marriage

This may surprise you, but the primary purpose of marriage is not to procreate. Couples who cannot bear children are just as married as couples who can. As Jesus said in Matthew 19:5, again quoting from Genesis 2, "'Therefore a man shall leave his father and his mother and hold fast to his wife, and the two shall become one flesh.'"

With that understanding, the boy that grew up to be a man and the girl that grew up to be a woman are to *leave their mothers and their fathers*. The preeminent relationship in a family is not between a child and a parent, but between a husband and a wife. The husband is specifically told to "hold fast" to his wife.

And the *two*, in God's divine arithmetic, become *one*. When God sees a parent and a child, he sees *two*. When God sees a brother and a sister, he sees *two*. When God sees a husband and a wife, he sees *one*.

That math lesson sets the stage for the answer Jesus is going to give to these Pharisees' wily question.

A *prime* number is also called an *indivisible* number. A prime number is a number that cannot be divided by any number except itself and one. The prime indivisible number of all numbers is *one*. You can divide *two* into separate whole pieces, but you can't divide *one*.

Talk about a game changer.

Commit to God's Permanence for Marriage

Did you know that the words you often hear at weddings before "you may now kiss the bride" aren't the preacher's *opinion*? Jesus concludes this teaching on marriage by saying, "What therefore God has joined together, let not man separate" (Matthew 19:6).

The phrase "joined together" means "to be glued to"—"What God has glued together, let no man separate." Do you ever feel like you are stuck with the person you are married to? You are! Getting married and becoming one flesh is not what two people do for each other or even to each other, but what God does for and to them.

Marriage is not what culture joins together. It is not what nature joins together or what the law joins together or what sex joins together or even what love joins together. Marriage is what God joins together.

What has been done by God cannot be undone by humanity. Marriage is always the work of God; divorce is always the work of people—and only God has the right to separate what he has joined together. The good news is that, as the two who've become one look to the One who invented marriage, what God has joined together, God can *keep* together.

This Week's Prayer: *Lord, as a person who's married or as one who's single, I give thanks that you are the inventor of and the sustainer of marriage between a man and a woman.*

This Week's Question: How does God "seeing *one* when he looks at *two*" change the way you think about marriage?

37

Can One Become Two?

This week's Scriptures:

- Matthew 19:7-12
- Matthew 5:31-32
- 1 Corinthians 7:10-16
- Hebrews 13:4
- Malachi 2:13-16

A Holy Design

These days there seem to be two extreme views of divorce and remarriage.

Some people want to try to dumb down the standard for divorce. They maintain that God says *less* than what he actually says. These allow for divorce and remarriage for any reason. A common question is, "If my spouse is sloppy, lowers my self-esteem, has different goals than I do, differs in parenting philosophies, is a financial time bomb, or just makes my life miserable, does God expect me to spend the rest of my life with that person?" The popular answer is, "Of course not!"

On the other hand, you've got people who want to raise the bar *higher* than God did. They try to make God say more than he actually says about divorce and remarriage, and they forbid all divorce and all remarriage under any circumstance.

There are four positions we might take concerning divorce and remarriage:

- Divorce and remarriage are forbidden under all circumstances.
- Divorce is permitted in some circumstances, but remarriage is not.

- Divorce and remarriage are permitted in all circumstances.
- Divorce and remarriage are permitted only under certain circumstances.

The filter for sifting through these is what God says about *marriage*. Once you understand God's design for marriage, then it is easy to understand what God says about divorce and remarriage and why he said it.

One and Done

Jesus has already stated that the Divine Architect designed the house of marriage with only one door. There is a front door that says "Entrance." There is no back door that says "Exit." What is killing marriage in America is not divorce at the end of a marriage, but the attitude that people have at the beginning of a marriage. In the minds of many, if not most, couples who get married is the thought, *If it doesn't work out, we can always get a divorce. And if I want to, I can do it all over again with somebody else.* Jesus's attitude toward marriage is *one and done.*

The Pharisees recognized that the issue of divorce, sticky now and sticky then, was an ideal opportunity to trap Jesus. Their sting operation had begun in the fifth chapter of Matthew's Gospel, when they heard Jesus make this statement during his Sermon on the Mount:

> "But I say to you that everyone who divorces his wife, except on the ground of sexual immorality, makes her commit adultery, and whoever marries a divorced woman commits adultery" (Matthew 5:32).

That was the ammo they needed to stir the pot by pressing, "Is it lawful to divorce one's wife for any cause?" (Matthew 19:3).

Jesus ultimately answers their question, but when he gets through, they wish they had never asked him.

Know the Reason Behind Divorce

Jesus has presented an ironclad case for why marriage should be permanent. Then, using the Old Testament witness as leverage, the Pharisees test Jesus: "Why then did Moses command one to give a certificate of divorce and to send her away?" (Matthew 19:7).

The pivotal word in their scheme was *command*. And some may have been fooled by it. But listen to Jesus's response: "Because of your hardness of heart Moses allowed you to divorce your wives, but from the beginning it was not so" (Matthew 19:8). Jesus first corrects them by noting that Moses never commanded divorce; he permitted divorce. God never says a couple *must* divorce but *may* divorce under permissible circumstances.

Then Jesus answered their question. The reason divorce was ever allowed was because of what Jesus calls "hardness of heart." That phrase is only one word in the Greek language, a combination of the word *sclero* (from which we get the word *sclerosis*) and the word *cardia* (from which we get the word *cardiologist*). Atherosclerosis is hardening of the arteries. Stunningly, Jesus gives the reason behind divorce ultimately as being the hardening of the spiritual arteries. That is a hard heart.

Invariably, the root cause of all divorce is sin. There are no problems too big to solve, just people too little (or hard-hearted) to solve them. Marriage is a divine institution. Divorce is a human invention. God never commands nor commends divorce. In a divorce unfortunately everybody loses.

Though in my pastoral work I've never counseled divorce, I have suggested separation. I don't believe that women ought to stay in abusive situations, and sometimes a couple may need to separate for a time. But if divorce transpires, it is because of the hardness of our hearts, either hardness toward trusting God or obeying God.

Understand the Restriction on Divorce

Jesus answers the wily Pharisees, "And I say to you: whoever divorces his wife, except for sexual immorality, and marries another, commits adultery" (Matthew 19:9).

He's saying that if you divorce for any reason other than sexual immorality on the part of your spouse, and you remarry someone else, you commit adultery.

In the ancient Near East, women didn't have the same rights as men. Men could divorce their wives, but wives could not divorce their husbands. This is why Jesus was talking only to men. Today, he would address both spouses.

Here is the chain reaction of sin: Every time a husband divorces his wife (or vice versa) for any reason other than sexual immorality, he commits adultery if he remarries. The person he remarries commits adultery. If his spouse remarries, she commits adultery and the person she remarries commits adultery. So, an unbiblical divorce leads to multiplied adultery.

When two believers marry and become one flesh, the only thing that can break that one flesh bond is adultery.

That said, even if a spouse has been unfaithful, it doesn't have to lead to divorce. There are two things that mitigate what Jesus said. First, the guilty party confesses and repents. Second, the innocent party loves and forgives. If that doesn't take place, then here is what Jesus says: The innocent party can divorce and remarry. The guilty party cannot. The guilty party can get forgiveness, but he or she no longer has the freedom to remarry.

Accept the Reality of Divorce

You may be thinking that what Jesus said is unrealistic. You question whether you are forbidden from divorcing no matter how miserable you are, how different you and your spouse are, and no matter how big your marital problems may be, unless there has been adultery. But Jesus teaches no less.

Experts say by consensus that the three key components for holding a marriage together are:

1. Make up your mind to stay with it.
2. Actively work on the relationship.
3. Focus on your own behavior and attitude, not that of your spouse.

Whenever a ship's captain was heading into a battle where surrender was not an option, he would order that the "colors" be nailed to the mast. Having the flags nailed up high, there was no possibility of lowering them in the heat of the battle in order to surrender. When you go into a battle knowing surrender is not an option, then your only motivation is to fix your mind on how you can best win that battle.

If you are married, nail the flag of your marriage to the post of God's Word and God's will for your life. *Remember your battle is not with your mate—it is for your marriage.* Focus your heart and your mind, not on how you can get out of your marriage, but how you can stay true to your "I do" for the glory of God.

This Week's Prayer: *Lord, whether I am single or married, give me your passion for enduring covenant faithfulness, and teach me to love like you love.*

This Week's Question: How does Jesus's teaching on divorce challenge the ways you think about marriage?

Love: Can Two Stay One?

This week's Scriptures:

- John 13:34-35
- John 15:12-17
- 1 John 4:7-12
- Galatians 5:13-26
- 1 Corinthians 13:1-13

Real Love

On my first date with Teresa, I told her that I tell a girl I love her only if I want to marry her. I warned her, "If I tell you I love you, I am asking you to marry me."

The next night, on our second date, I told Teresa that I loved her. If I had been a comedian, I would have felt great, because I don't think she has quit laughing yet! But I was serious, and six months later we were married.

Since the wedding, we've had our problems. We haven't always seen eye-to-eye, and sometimes marriage has been more of a battle than a blessing. Yet, we've worked through problems, talked through disagreements, and persevered through conflict. And I have never loved her more than I do now. Our marriage hasn't been easy, but it reminds me that staying in love after you fall in love is possible.

There is a big difference between falling in love and staying in love. One takes a pulse and the other takes a commitment.

After thirty-seven years of marriage, I can testify that staying in love is not something that happens automatically, nor is it something that happens easily. Yet real love is the glue that holds a marriage together. It's the foundation of any relationship that endures. But the love Jesus spoke about is not what you read about in a romantic novel or see in some Hollywood fairy tale.

A Special Kind of Love

Everybody loves love. If you stood up in a meeting of people of different faiths, whether it be Christian, Muslim, Jewish, Buddhist, or Hindu, and said, "God is love," you wouldn't get any pushback at all. People like the idea of a God who is love. We are in love with the idea of love. We love "love" in America so much we even have an entire day called "Valentine's Day" devoted to expressing it. Still, when two people fall in love, why is it that many of them can't stay in love?

Tucked away in a Gospel is a little two-paragraph statement Jesus made that gives us the foundation for any enduring relationship. It speaks of the kind of love that is so strong that if a husband and wife have it, nothing can break it.

Jesus wasn't even talking about marriage when he said this. He wasn't talking to spouses; he was talking to disciples. What Jesus said to believers, generally, I am going to apply to marriage specifically. Jesus exhorts his disciples,

> "A new commandment I give to you, that you love one another:
> just as I have loved you, you also are to love one another. By this
> all people will know that you are my disciples, if you have love
> for one another" (John 13:34-35).

He's saying something about the *kind* of love that lasts, isn't he? It's not the Hollywood version of love. Rather, Jesus is saying: *you stay in love with a love from above.*

Obeying the Command of Jesus

Love is not an emotion. You cannot *command* a feeling—but Jesus does command us to love. Love may express itself emotionally, warming or stirring your tummy. It may make your heart beat faster, but none of those are the signs of real love.

Liking someone is a feeling. And there is a big difference between liking people and loving people. Jesus never commands us to like our enemies. You can't command someone to *like* somebody else. Liking someone is purely an emotional response. It's the way we felt the first time we heard Taylor Swift strum a guitar or saw Rachel walk into Central Perk on *Friends* or caught a glimpse of the unique Marilyn Monroe.

Loving is an action. I don't have to like someone to love them, and I love people I don't necessarily like. The truth is not everybody that loves you is going to like you.

If love were an emotion, Jesus would never have died on the cross, because in the Garden of Gethsemane, we see he didn't feel like dying on the cross. Emotions ride on roller coasters—up one day and down the next. Love rides on a railroad track across the Central Plains—always straight, always level, and never off course.

Following the Model of Jesus

Though the Old Testament talks about love, Jesus calls this a "new commandment." How is it new exactly?

What's new is this bit: "just as I have loved you." He's commanding us to love each other the way we've been loved. Here, "just as" is a causative phrase, which means the verse could be translated, "You are to give love to others from the love that I have given to you." If you are a follower of Jesus, you not only have Jesus in you, but you have the *love* of Jesus in you and you are to love your spouse with *that love*.

For three years, Jesus always put his disciples first—washing their feet, saving them from a storm, patiently teaching them. Jesus put them first. He didn't look out for number one. He looked out for the Twelve.

C.S. Lewis suggests how he came to view others' faults differently:

> There is someone I love even though I don't approve of what he does. There is someone I accept, though some of his thoughts and actions revolt me. There is someone I forgive though he hurts the people I love the most. That person is *me*...if I can love myself without approving of all I do, I can also love others without approving of all they do.[13]

Giving a Witness for Jesus

If you and your spouse claim to be followers of Jesus, there is far more at stake in loving one another and far more at stake in holding your marriage together than just the welfare of the children or even just staying true to your vow. What is at stake is your witness before the world.

> "By this all people will know that you are my disciples, if you have love for one another" (John 13:35).

That's how the world will know that this thing called Christianity is a game changer! One of the greatest witnesses a married couple can give to their neighbors is to stay married, to work through their problems, to hang in the battle, to refuse to surrender, and to keep loving one another.

In the early days of the church, the emperor Hadrian sent a man named Aristides to spy out these strange creatures known as Christians. Having seen them in action, Aristides returned to the emperor with his report. Since then, these immortal words have echoed down through history: "Behold! How they love one another."

Whatever else is said about you, your spouse, and your marriage, let your children and grandchildren, friends, relatives, and neighbors say, "Behold! How they love one another." That is how two can stay one.

This Week's Prayer: *Lord, teach me to love from the love with which you've already loved me. May others know that your Gospel is true because of the way I love.*

This Week's Question: Who do you look to as an example of someone who loves the way Jesus has loved them?

39

The Number One Priority

This week's Scriptures:

- Matthew 6:25-33
- Philippians 3:7-14
- Mark 10:28-31
- Matthew 16:24-27
- Acts 28:23-31

Ordering Our Priorities

A few days after the story of Tiger Woods's infidelity broke, I was watching my favorite television network—one that's informational, educational, inspirational. That's right, I was watching ESPN. The hostess was interviewing Herman Edwards, a former NFL coach, and she asked him, "So what do you think happened with Tiger Woods?"

Without hesitation Edwards replied, "Tiger simply had his priorities in the wrong place."

Edwards's wisdom resonates, doesn't it? The constructive power of proper priorities can take any ordinary life and turn it into an extraordinary adventure. The destructive power of misplaced priorities can take an ordinary life and crush it into a million pieces.

Life offers every one of us hundreds, and if you live long enough thousands, of possibilities. Some are bad, many are good, and there are a few that are the best. Each one of us, as we make choices and decisions, has to ask, "What priority takes first place in my life?"

The answer will guide the choices you make. And, ultimately, the sum total of your life will be determined by what you choose to make your greatest priority.

You *Can* Get What You Want

I'm reading a book right now by a *New York Times* best-selling author on how to be successful. He says the key to getting from where you are to where you want to be is to know where you are now and where you want to be. His whole approach is summed up in a quote he gives from Ben Stein, the actor and author, who said, "The indispensable first step to getting the things you want out of life is this: decide what you want." This book is all about how to get it done, how to climb the ladder, how to make the money, and how to be successful.

What Jesus Christ has to say about priorities is different from what this man, and what most business leaders, have to say:

"But seek first his kingdom and his righteousness, and all these things will be given to you as well" (Matthew 6:33 NIV).

If you're still weighing who you'll trust on this issue of priorities, Jesus's wisdom even comes with a guarantee: if you make his priority your priority, everything else will fall into place. *The key to getting what you need out of life is to focus on what Jesus wants for your life.* The indispensable first step to getting everything you need is to focus on what Jesus wants.

This book I'm reading spends 435 pages telling me how to get what I want out of life. Jesus used one sentence.

I Must Experience a Connection with God in My Life

Jesus's first two words are critical: "Seek first."

Seek means "to strive for diligently" or "to desire strongly." The action is continuous. It says, "keep on striving for," "keep on seeking," and "keep on desiring daily."

When Jesus says, "Seek first God's kingdom and God's righteousness," it means we don't even have to pray about what our top priority ought to be. If my number one priority in life is to seek God's kingdom and God's righteousness, then everything I do can be ordered by two things. Where I work, how I spend my time, the person I marry, how I manage my money, what I buy always have to be sifted and sorted through one filter: "Is this for his kingdom? Does it relate to his righteousness?"

Do you understand how this could transform your marriage, your work, your family, and your finances?

In order to seek the kingdom, of course, you have to first seek the King—because you won't even know where the kingdom is or what it looks like until you know the King. Seek a connection with Christ daily by reading his Word, letting him speak to you, and responding to him in prayer.

I Must Establish the Control of God over My Life

Every kingdom has a king and every king has a throne. That throne is the seat of authority from which the king rules and reigns. In a kingdom, the king's word is the only word that matters. And subjects of a kingdom do the will of the king.

Your heart is a throne. Someone is going to sit on the throne and rule over your life. At any given moment, there will always be one of two people on that throne: you or Jesus. In every decision that you make, either *you* will decide to do what you want to do or you will decide to do what *God* wants you to do. The moment that you decide to do what you want to do instead of what God wants you to do, your priorities just got scrambled like eggs.

If you are pursuing the rule of the King, then you will be seeking three things. You will seek the glory of the King. You will seek the guidance of the King. And you will also seek the governace of the King.

But perhaps you're wondering, "When do I get what *I* want?"

Here's the beauty of it: when you decide that you want whatever the King wants in your life, then you will always get what you want.

I Must Exhibit the Character of God in My Life

One of the fascinating stories from April 15, 1912, the night the RMS *Titanic* sank killing more than fifteen hundred people, is one about priorities.

A frightened woman was in a lifeboat that was about to be lowered into the North Atlantic. She suddenly thought of something she needed, so she asked permission to return to her stateroom before they cast off. They gave her three minutes or they would have to leave without her.

She ran across the deck that was already slanted at a dangerous angle and raced through the gambling room, where all the money had rolled to one side and was ankle deep. She came to her stateroom and pushed aside all her expensive jewelry, reached up to the shelf above her bed, and grabbed three small oranges. Then she found her way back to the lifeboat.

Can you believe that she bypassed money, diamonds, and gold for three small oranges? At that moment, that lady had her priorities in order.

We all live on a ship called "Titanic," and that ship is sinking slowly every day. One day it will be submerged completely under the water of death, and all that will matter then will be this: Did you make the right choices? Did you make the right decisions? Did you have the right priorities?

As you seek to order your life, remember that Christ and his kingdom should be in first place.

This Week's Prayer: *Lord, quicken in my heart a greater desire to seek after your kingdom. Give me the will to desire, above all else, that your will be done.*

This Week's Question: As you bow to God's will, what of *your* will do you need to release?

Jesus, the Helper

One of Jesus's most endearing qualities was the way he proactively pursued the outcast and outsider. He was a man of the people, not just the privileged. He was a master for the masses, not a rabbi for the rich. Jesus sought out those that society avoided, mocked, and ridiculed. He was willing to help anyone at any time—even if they didn't realize they needed him. Jesus's most scandalous encounters reveal his role as a helper of the helpless and the hope of the hopeless, all the while changing the way we see others and ourselves.

40

The Thirst Quencher

This week's Scriptures:

- John 4:1-42
- Revelation 22:17
- Isaiah 55:1-5

- John 7:37-39
- Revelation 7:14-17

Messy Mess Ups

In 2006, Alitalia Airlines made a slight mistake on its website. They advertised business-class seats from Toronto to Cyprus for $39. The price was supposed to be $3900, but an employee left off two zeros. Customers bought two thousand tickets, and it cost the airline $7.7 million.

Somebody messed up.

Maybe you have messed up and are living under the crushing burden of that mess up. Hear this clearly: just because you have messed up doesn't mean you have to stay messed up.

The apostle John tells the story of an amazing encounter between Jesus and a messed-up woman (John 4). And it's the longest conversation ever recorded between Jesus and any other individual.

When you first read the story, it seems mundane and ordinary. A woman, whose name we never know, is performing the most boring, everyday task: drawing water out of a well. She'd come all by herself. And where no other man would have given her the time of day, except for the wrong reasons, Jesus engages her in a conversation that will radically change her life.

This woman's encounter with Jesus not only demonstrates how we should relate to people who are on the fringe, but it's also a wonderful gift for all of us who have messed up at one time or another. What we discover from this woman who doesn't deny her messy past is that as we fess up to our mess ups, Jesus will clean up our messes.

We Should Know that Jesus Is Waiting to Meet Us

Jesus is not at just any well, but *Jacob's* well in Samaria. Anyone in John's audience would immediately know where this was. This was a field that Jacob had purchased thousands of years earlier so that he could pitch his tent in the land of Canaan. This was the first piece of real estate recorded in the Bible that any Jew ever owned in the Promised Land.

If you think it would be a natural place for Jesus to visit, though, you'd be wrong.

Jews never, *ever* went through Samaria. They considered it the other side of the tracks. Any self-respecting Jew would always take a detour, even if it added a day's journey, to keep from going through Samaria.

The sixth hour was at high noon, and a woman, alone, comes to draw water. Any onlooker's eyebrows would have gone through the ceiling. Middle Eastern village women would always avoid the heat of the day, getting water either early in the morning or just before sundown. And for the sake of propriety, they would always go as a group. Because the jars were heavy when they were full and difficult for a woman to lift onto her head alone, they would help each other carry the water back to their homes. We know this Samaritan woman is an outcast because she comes at the worst time of the day and arrives alone. The "woman at the well" is also a woman on the fringe.

Someone Wants to Meet You

Jesus is sitting on top of the well. As a man, he was expected to withdraw to a distance of at least twenty feet, indicating it was both safe and appropriate for her to come to the well. But Jesus doesn't move. He is waiting to meet her.

In that day, a man, particularly a stranger, not only would not talk to a woman, but he wouldn't even make eye contact with her. Not only does Jesus break the sexual barrier when he speaks to her, he breaks the racial barrier. He ignores a seven-hundred-year hostility that had been going on between Jews and Samaritans.

The woman is shocked and thinks, *Are you blind? Not only am I a woman, but I am also a Samaritan!*

And that's just the point. Jesus chose this time, this place, and this woman to have one of the greatest conversations he would ever have.

And just as he waited for this woman, he is waiting to meet us. Jesus is not the least bit bothered by who you are, what you've done, or what anybody else thinks of you.

We Should Believe that Jesus Is Willing to Accept Us

Here is a Jewish man speaking with respect to a Samaritan woman and letting her know he would be honored to drink from her filthy, sin-contaminated, Samaritan jug. For the first time in her life, a man was looking at her not with the eyes of lust but with the eyes of love.

Then, on a dime, Jesus turns the entire conversation around. At first, he was thirsty and she had the water, but now he is about to show her she is the thirsty one and he is the One with the water.

Jesus gently reveals what they both know: she was a Samaritan woman married five times who was now living with a man who wasn't even her husband. We don't know why she had been married five times. Maybe her husbands died. Maybe her marriages ended in divorce. Maybe the woman couldn't have children. We aren't told. But like a fly in a spider's web, she has been caught.

She expects to be judged, but what ensues is a conversation about worshipping God. And what she discovers is that anybody, no matter what they've done or who they are, no matter how bad they have messed up, can worship God if they do it in spirit and in truth.

We Should Rejoice that Jesus Wants to Change Us

Then the conversation hits an astonishing climax. Jesus's words are far more powerful in Greek, because what he said was, "The One who is speaking to you is 'I am'" (John 4:26).

Anybody who knew the Old Testament would know that *I am* is what God called himself in the Old Testament. Jesus is claiming to be God. Never before in any biblical record had he ever come out so blatantly to anyone and declared exactly who he was. And he doesn't do it to a Jew, but he does it to a Samaritan! He doesn't even do it to a Samaritan man, but to a Samaritan woman. He doesn't even do it to a self-respecting, clean, pure Samaritan woman, but to a five-time married woman living with a man not her husband. In that instant, believing she was changed, she dropped her water jug and went running into town to preach to her friends.

Jesus didn't *have* to go through Samaria. Yet he chose to go to an out-of-the-way town to extend God's grace and love to an out-of-the-way woman—one who discovered she'd been thirsty because she'd been drinking the wrong kind of water.

This Week's Prayer: *Lord, teach me to see others the way you see them—as being worthy of time, attention, and living water. Show me, this week, who is thirsty for you.*

This Week's Question: Do you remember what it's like to be desperately thirsty for the One who truly satisfies?

41

A Most Valuable Treasure

This week's Scriptures:

- Mark 10:17-22
- Romans 12:1-2
- Titus 3:4-8
- Ecclesiastes 5:10-20
- Ezekiel 18:4-9

Losers Who Win, Winners Who Lose

Several years ago, *The Biggest Loser* debuted on national television, and it has fascinated millions of viewers ever since. If you have never seen the show, it's about people who compete with other contestants to win a grand prize of a quarter of a million dollars by losing the highest percentage of body weight in a certain period of time.

Those of you who *have* watched the show may know the name Michael Ventrella. He was the biggest loser on season nine of the program. This thirtysomething Chicago DJ set several records in his quest to lose weight.

He weighed in at a record 526 pounds. By the end of his contest, he had lost a record 264 pounds. He lost 50.19 percent of his body weight! In other words, at the end of the show, he was literally half the man he used to be.

Mark's Gospel describes Jesus's encounter with an even bigger loser— perhaps the biggest loser of all time (Mark 10:17-22)! Jesus moved toward a lot of people that nobody else wanted to encounter: the failures, the rejects, the desperate, the losers. But this guy? Both financially and spiritually, he could have had it all. And yet he wound up with nothing. He could have been the biggest winner but instead became the biggest loser.

A Rich Young Ruler

Matthew, Mark, and Luke call this guy wealthy; Matthew says he was young; Luke tells us he was a ruler. So he's often referred to as "the rich young ruler."

He was rich. If he lived today he would be wearing Italian shoes, a tailored suit, his money invested in blue-chip stocks. He would carry only platinum credit cards and fly his own jet.

He was young. In his culture that meant he was under forty. He had his whole life ahead of him. He worked out daily and was in great shape and perfect health.

He was a ruler. He was either a magistrate or he worked in the office of the high priest. He was respected and at least outwardly righteous.

So how did he wind up the biggest loser?

Because the most important thing anyone will ever have in life was something he could not purchase with his money, achieve through his influence, or attain through his connections. He didn't understand that sacrifice is key to having a relationship with Christ. This big loser could have been the biggest winner if only he had realized that *in order to go up, you have to give up.*

Desire the Gift of Eternal Life

This man runs up to Jesus and asks, "Good Teacher, what must I do to inherit eternal life?" (Mark 10:17).

He is not ashamed for anybody to hear his conversation and he *kneels* before Jesus. Here is a ruler kneeling at the feet of a carpenter. Here is management kneeling at the feet of labor. This crowd knew who this man was, and they were shocked that he would be kneeling before anybody.

Why was he so adamant? Because in his heart was this burning desire: he wanted eternal life. He realized there had to be more to life than what he was experiencing. When he looked at his life, he realized there was a piece of the puzzle missing: "I am not firing on all eight cylinders."

Daniel Webster, the brilliant statesman and lawyer, was once asked, "What is the greatest thought that has ever passed through your mind?" Webster replied, "The greatest thought that has ever passed through my mind is the thought that one day I'm going to have to stand before God. I am going to have to give an account of my life before God."

This young man had realized that one day he was going to meet God, and he wanted to make sure he was ready.

He asks Jesus a question, and Jesus gives the answer the man is expecting: you can have eternal life if you keep all the commandments.

Determine the Cost of Eternal Life

Are you surprised at Jesus's answer? What about grace? What about faith? And yet his answer is true: if anybody could keep all of the commandments and never sin, they would be sinless, they would be perfect, and they would have eternal life. But except for Jesus, no one has ever done that and no one ever will.

Mark explains, "And Jesus, looking at him, loved him, and said to him, 'You lack one thing: go, sell all that you have and give to the poor, and you will have treasure in heaven; and come, follow me'" (Mark 10:21). Jesus looked at this young man and *felt love* for him. This man was serious and sincere, and Jesus loved him enough to tell him the truth.

Remember, this man came to Jesus because, even though he had kept the law on the outside, he knew something was wrong on the inside. This man came face-to-face with the fact that his money was his master. Gold was his god. Silver was his savior.

And what Jesus was saying was, "If you want God in your heart, you've got to give your heart to God."

Decide to Pay the Price for Eternal Life

That the man went away disheartened can feel confusing. This guy is rich. You don't go away sad because you are rich. You go away sad because you are driving a thirty-five-year-old, four-cylinder Ford Pinto! Why would walking away with all these riches make him sad? Here's why: this man came face-to-face with the realization that what he owned owned him.

After Christian fighters captured Jerusalem during the First Crusade, pilgrims from all over Western Europe began visiting the Holy Land. Around AD 1100, a French knight formed an organization called the

Knights Templar. Their job was to protect these pilgrims during their visit. When these knights were baptized by the church, they brought their swords with them. But the knights didn't take their swords under water with them. Instead, they held their swords up out of the water while they were immersed. They were saying to Jesus, "You can have control of all of me, except this one part. I am all yours, except when I am on the battlefield. All that I have is yours, except this sword."

When people today get baptized they don't hold up a sword, but they hold up their wallets. Their laptops. Deeds to their homes. Their 401(k)s. They hold up their pride, their egos, their bitterness, their grudges.

Only when you surrender everything to Jesus can you avoid becoming the biggest loser and let him transform you into the biggest winner.

This Week's Prayer: *Lord, everything I have is yours. Open my eyes to the way I've held my goods and my life back from you. Lord, I surrender all.*

This Week's Question: Using the eyes of your heart, what are you holding up and keeping dry above the baptismal waters?

42

A Gracious Judge

This week's Scriptures:

- John 8:1-11
- 1 John 1:5-10
- Romans 6:15-23
- Matthew 18:15-20
- Ephesians 4:29-32

Caught in the Act

A mother had been working with her young son trying to teach him to tell time using a nondigital clock. For several days she kept talking to him about the "little hand" and the "big hand." One day she heard him walk into the kitchen, where there was a clock on the wall, with the big hand and the little hand on the face.

She called from the other room, "Cameron, what is the little hand on?"

He yelled back, "A chocolate-chip cookie!"

If you are into legalese, you may have come across the legal term *in flagrante delicto*. In Latin it means "while the crime is blazing." It indicates that a criminal has been caught in the very act of committing an offense. One might say, "Caught red-handed."

Whether you say it in Latin or in English, nothing could be more humiliating, embarrassing, or shameful than to be caught red-handed. That may mean being caught in a compromising situation in the backseat of a car or stealing money from your company or, as I was, trying to cheat on a high-school chemistry exam.

If you have any conscience at all, any character at all, when you are caught red-handed with no escape and no excuse, it will leave you broken.

For the Broken

John recounts a story about a woman who was not just broken but ashamed and afraid (John 8). She was ashamed because she had been caught having sexual relations with a man who was not her husband. And because she'd been caught, she was afraid of what was probably going to happen to her.[14]

Every one of us is in this sordid story. If you are a religious person, you are in the story. If you are an extremely nonreligious person, you are in the story. If you are a conservative and you believe that sin should be dealt with in a straightforward way, there is something for you to learn. If you are a liberal and you think that sin should be dealt with in a tolerant way, there is something for you to learn.

Most importantly, if you have ever blown it, failed, taken the wrong road, made the wrong choice, or gotten caught in the act, and you are broken, this story demonstrates how Jesus takes brokenness and turns it into blessing.

Come to Jesus, He Will Give You Grace

This story takes place early in the morning, and Jesus is actually teaching a Bible study. The scribes and the Pharisees burst into this Bible study, dragging a woman behind them who had been caught in the act of adultery. Their concern wasn't for this woman. She was just a pawn on the chessboard of this confrontation.

These Pharisees think they've caught Jesus in a trap and the air is thick with anticipation.

Oddly, Jesus bends down and writes on the ground with his finger.

What was he writing? We can only speculate, but since the Greek word John chooses for "write" means "to write against," I suspect that Jesus was writing down the sins these Pharisees and scribes were guilty of! Maybe the first word he wrote was *hypocrisy*. As he doodled, one by one these Pharisees left.

It reminds me of Sir Arthur Conan Doyle, author of the Sherlock Holmes mysteries, who loved practical jokes. One time, just as a practical joke, he sent a telegram to twelve of his friends, all highly respected and well known. The anonymous telegram said, "Flee at once. Your secret has been discovered!"

Within twenty-four hours, all twelve had left the country.

Though that story may be legendary, the one John relays is not. The Pharisees were in the rock-throwing business. Jesus was in the sin-healing business. They were in the guilt business and Jesus was in the grace business.

Confess to Jesus, He Will Remove Your Guilt

The first word out of Jesus's mouth let this woman know that he was completely different from any other man she'd ever met. For starters, he uses the term *woman* when he addresses her. Unlike today, the name was one of respect, the way we might use *lady* today. Jesus used the same word in speaking to his own mother while on the cross.

When this woman hears this voice of tenderness and kindness, she is all ears, wondering what Jesus is going to say to her. And he says those magic words that were music to her ears—and ours: "I don't condemn you."

How I wish I had a picture of the look on that woman's face at this moment. Jesus and this woman are left alone. The jury has gone, and all of a sudden she has gone from the courtroom to the judge's chambers. She is awaiting the verdict, which she knows will be *guilty*. But the Judge says, "I don't condemn you."

If you have ever wondered how God reacts when you fail, when you blow it, when you mess up, when you are guilty, then you ought to frame these words and hang them on the wall of your heart.

Commit to Jesus, He Will Lead You to Goodness

We've all heard the saying many times, "God loves the sinner, but he hates the sin." That is a theologically true statement. This woman's sin was forgiven, but her sin was not *excused*. Jesus doesn't just wink at this sin. He doesn't just say, "Boys will be boys and that's all right." He doesn't condemn *her*, but he does condemn her sin.

Not only do we have the right to condemn whatever the Bible condemns, we have the responsibility to do so. Condemning sin is not the same as judging the sinner. Jesus said two things to this woman, and they both go together: "Woman, I don't condemn you, but I do condemn what you did. Go and do it no more."

Jesus loves us just the way we are, but he loves us too much to let us stay that way. Condemning sinners is not my job or yours. But condemning sin is.

Jesus gives us grace and removes our guilt so he can lead us to goodness. When this woman encountered Jesus, when she received grace and repented of her sin, her brokenness was turned into blessing. And you're invited to let Jesus do the same for you.

This Week's Prayer: *Lord, show me where I am in this story of your grace. Transform my life as I turn away from whatever sin is keeping me from you.*

This Week's Question: Where do you find yourself in this story? Clenching rocks or exposed as a broken sinner?

43

Always Available, Always Accessible

This week's Scriptures:

- Mark 5:25-34
- Hebrews 4:14-16
- Mark 10:13-16
- Matthew 19:13-15
- Luke 18:35-42

Close Enough to Touch

Have you ever gotten close to someone famous or someone you admired, and you just wanted to reach out and touch them? I have.

A friend and I went to Augusta National Golf Club to watch the Masters Tournament. We were standing in a rope line that was only about three-feet wide, a corridor where players walked from one tee to the next. I looked up and here came a young phenom who had taken the golf world by storm. His name was Tiger Woods. My heart was about to come out of my chest. He got one foot from me, and I started to reach out to pat him on the shoulder when he looked me square in the eyes, as if to say, "Don't you even think about it."

Later I thought about how foolish I had been and how stupid I felt. I didn't want his autograph or a conversation, I just wanted to reach out and touch his shirt.

Since then I've wondered how many times I have been surrounded by people who just needed to know that I was aware they were there, that somebody cared about them, but I was too focused on the game I was playing to pay any attention.

The fifth chapter of Mark's Gospel describes a woman who came to know, beyond a shadow of a doubt, that someone noticed her and cared about her.

Encountering One Who Helps

Traveling with his disciples, Jesus is in the midst of a bustling crowd. People are pushing and shoving just to get a look at him, just to be able to tell their grandchildren that they saw Jesus. Parents are holding up their children so they can see him. Perhaps there are people who, like Zacchaeus, have climbed trees just to look into his face.

Along the "rope line," caught up in the bustle of the crowd, is a woman with a terrible disease that's sapping the life out of her. A continuous flow of blood is slowly but surely killing her. In all the pushing and shoving, no one notices the little woman who is weak, sick, and shy. Gingerly, but purposefully, she is pressing her way through the crowd with steely determination.

When she reaches out in faith to touch the hem of Jesus's garment, her bleeding is instantaneously stopped. In addition to a physical miracle, it was an emotional and spiritual miracle.

This woman needed what all hurting people need: help and hope. Jesus offered her both. And as we pattern our lives after Jesus, he brings us people who hurt so that we can offer them help and hope.

We Need to Give Hurting People the Addition of Our Presence

The desperate woman had a chronic menstrual disorder. She'd been bleeding for twelve years. She was physically exhausted, socially ostracized, and mentally drained. She had sought help, but "had suffered a great deal under the care of many doctors" (Mark 5:26 NIV). The Talmud, an ancient Jewish writing, gives eleven different cures for the condition this woman had. She had tried every one of them and nothing had happened. On top of all this, she was financially bankrupt. She "had spent all she had." Yet everyday she woke up to a body that no one wanted. Every day she woke up to a life that was lonely. I believe the greatest pain this woman suffered was the pain of isolation.

She didn't need a cure. She needed compassion. She needed the presence of someone in her life who was willing to take time out of their busy schedule to let her know "I care about you" and "I'll be here to help you."

There are people all around us like this woman. They are made fun of, ridiculed, and isolated, and they need someone's presence in their life.

We Need to Give Hurting People the Attention of Our Minds

Jesus is on his way to help the dying daughter of a man named Jairus, a synagogue ruler, who was the most important man in that community. Everybody wanted to get close to Jesus, but Jairus had first dibs. No one wanted to cross him. One word from him and you could be kicked out of the synagogue, blacklisted.

What are the odds that Jesus would interrupt an urgent mission with the most important man in the community to help a financially bankrupt, social outcast like this woman? If this crowd had found out who she was, they would have fled from her because she was considered unclean.

She decided to take that risk because somebody had told her about Jesus. Somebody had cared enough to say to her, "I know somebody who can help you."

She believed them, because she reached out and touched the hem of Jesus's garment.

Whenever his garment is touched—whether by the hand of a severely anemic woman in Galilee or by the pleas of a homeless person near you today—Jesus stops. Jesus responds. Jesus lets that hurting person know, "You are not unimportant because of what you don't have; instead, you are important because of who you are."

We Need to Give Hurting People the Affection of Our Hearts

When this woman touched Jesus Christ, two things happened that had never happened before in the Bible and never happened again in the Bible.

First, Jesus heals someone seemingly unaware. When this woman touched the hem of his garment, power was automatically and instantaneously released. What triggered his help was her need. That is the way God operates.

Also, this is the only time anywhere that Jesus addresses any woman as "daughter." Most likely this woman couldn't remember the last time anybody had offered her a kind word. She could not remember the last time anybody looked at her with anything but dismay and disgust. Yet, with a look of love that only Jesus could give, he tenderly calls her "daughter."

Leo Tolstoy, the great Russian writer, tells of the time he was walking down the street and passed a beggar. He reached into his pocket to get the beggar some money, but his pocket was empty. He felt bad. Rather than just ignore the man and keep walking, he turned to the man and said, "I am so sorry, my brother, that I don't have anything to give you." The beggar's face widened into a smile the size of a half moon. He said, "Mister, you have given me more than I could have ever asked for: you have called me 'brother.'"

You and I are called to do the same, to minister the grace, the love, and the power of Jesus Christ—to be the hem of his garment.

This Week's Prayer: *Lord, give me the faith of a woman who believed in your power to heal, and allow me to minister in your name to those who hurt.*

This Week's Question: If you know Jesus, are you telling others about him so that they, too, can be healed?

44

Our Best Friend

This week's Scriptures:

- Luke 19:1-10
- Luke 7:31-34
- Matthew 9:9-13

- 1 Timothy 1:12-17
- Micah 4:6-7

Rejected by Others

By all appearances twenty-one-year-old Vicky Harrison was a beautiful, perky blonde with a sweet personality, great ambition, and a seemingly bright future. Tragically, she killed herself after more than two-hundred unsuccessful job applications. She had dreamed of a career as a teacher or a television producer, but gave up hope for the future. She wrote heartbreaking notes to her parents and boyfriend saying, "I don't want to be me anymore," and took a huge drug overdose and died. She could no longer live with the thought of rejection.

Someone who also experienced rejection was a man named Zacchaeus. His story is found in Luke 19. Luke tells us that Zacchaeus was a chief tax collector. He was a thief and he was a traitor. His family had disowned him, his friends had deserted him, and everybody despised him. He was hated and ostracized because of what he had done. Unlike Vicky, unlike many, his rejection—ironically—had been earned *honestly*.

The name Zacchaeus means "pure" or "innocent." Zacchaeus was anything but that. He was dirty and he was guilty. Anyone in his community would have known who he was and known about his sordid reputation. And, whenever possible, they would have steered clear of this scoundrel.

Reasonable Rejection

Taxes were collected at three places in Israel: Capernaum, Jericho, and Jerusalem. Jericho, seventeen miles northeast of Jerusalem, was by far the most lucrative. A border city set at an international crossroads, this was a place where the northern, southern, eastern, and western highway routes all converged.

Zacchaeus wasn't just *a* tax collector. He was a *chief* tax collector. In other words, he had tax collectors working under him. He was like the CEO of a tax-collecting corporation, and he had people under him who went out and did the dirty work, and then they paid him the greatest part of the profit. He was the godfather. He was the chief thief of the Roman IRS and in cahoots with the Roman government.

In first-century culture, a chief tax collector was considered no better than a murderer, reprobate, and robber. Tax collectors would bid for the position knowing that, no matter how high the bid, they would more than make it up. They would be given a quota of taxes to collect, but they were not limited to that quota. They made money by adding a surcharge or a user's fee, if you will. That surcharge could be as high as they wanted it to be—and their neighbors had to pay it!

Then Jesus came to town, demonstrating both how we can reach out to the rejected and what happens to the rejected when they receive Jesus.

We Must Be Attractive to Those Who Feel Rejected

The whole city had turned out to see Jesus. The streets were jammed. All the front seats were gone. Standing room only.

Zacchaeus, probably not even five feet tall, runs and climbs up the branches of a sycamore tree to see Jesus. This detail seems minor to us, but turns out to be significant. In the first century, it was considered undignified and even obscene for a man to climb a tree. But this chief tax collector set aside his dignity in order to see Jesus.

Why was he so determined? Maybe because Jesus had developed quite the reputation. People were calling him a glutton and a drunkard, a friend of tax collectors and sinners (Luke 7:34). People who felt unloved by everybody else felt loved by Jesus.

The more those who are not followers of Christ are loved by those of us who are followers of Christ, the more open they may be to following Christ. Specifically, we should be attractive to them by the way we love them, by the way we respect them, and by the way we treat them.

We Must Be Attracted to Those Who Feel Rejected

Zacchaeus appears in the Bible not because he was looking for Jesus but because Jesus was looking for him. If Jesus had passed by that tree and never looked up, we would have never even known who Zacchaeus was. Jesus found the guy trying to find him!

Jesus beckoned, "Zacchaeus, hurry and come down, for I must stay at your house today" (Luke 19:5). He didn't say, "I would like to stay at your house," but "I must stay at your house. I want to stay at your house. I am going to stay at your house."

This was a man who always ate Thanksgiving dinner alone. When he cooked out, he needed only one steak because nobody else would eat with him. This is the only time we are ever told that Jesus invited himself to be someone's guest, and yet he chose a chief tax collector.

Jesus could have stayed with anybody. Anybody would have gladly accepted Jesus, but Jesus didn't ask the mayor of the city, the president of the bank, the rabbi of the mega-synagogue, or the chief of police. He reached out to the reject.

We Must Be Attentive to Those Who Feel Rejected

We are not told what happened at Zacchaeus's house. We don't know whether Jesus got to eat dinner or even spent the night. We don't know what they talked about. But whatever else happened that day, Zacchaeus was convicted and converted (Luke 19:8-9). Jesus was attentive to his greatest need. His greatest need was not to be accepted by the town or accepted by others. His greatest need was to accept Christ.

According to the law, if a thief voluntarily confessed to stealing something, he had to restore only what he had stolen plus 20 percent interest. Zacchaeus was so changed, he vowed to return much more than was due.

Imagine you answer a knock at your door and see Zacchaeus. With anger flashing in your eyes you say, "You little thief! What do you want?"

"Do you know how much I have taken from you over the years?" he says.

"Yes, a hundred shekels!"

He checks his books and says, "You're right, a hundred shekels. Here is your hundred shekels, plus four hundred shekels more. Does that make us square?"

"What...what has happened to you?"

That wee little man smiles and, with tears in his eyes, says, "I met Jesus and I have learned that God receives the rejected and he rejoices over their repentance."

When Jesus comes into your life he not only makes you right with him, but he also makes you want to be right with others.

This Week's Prayer: *Lord, give me your vision to notice and care for those who are rejected. Help me to move toward those that you love on the world's fringes.*

This Week's Question: Who are the ones in your life, right now, who feel rejected?

Jesus, the Leader

Few words are batted about by managers, pastors, entrepreneurs, and politicians more than *leadership*. When we want to learn how to lead, we often look to those whose names emblazon book covers and fancy business cards. But what about the leader who claims more followers than any person in history? What made Jesus such a great leader? The answer has the power to transform us into people of influence and impact.

45

The Standard of Greatness

This week's Scriptures:

- Mark 9:30-35
- Matthew 20:20-28
- 1 Peter 4:7-11
- Philippians 2:1-8
- 1 Corinthians 9:19-23

Who's the Greatest?

If you want to get a discussion going anytime, anywhere, anyplace, just ask, "Who is the greatest _____ of all time?" You are bound to get some animated conversation, if not a heated argument.

For example, who is the greatest president of all time? Many would say Abraham Lincoln. Others would say George Washington. Still others would say Franklin Delano Roosevelt.

Who is the greatest golfer of all time? Some would say, "Without a doubt, Tiger Woods." He is the only golfer who has held all four major titles at the same time though he hasn't won as many major titles as Jack Nicklaus. Who is the greatest basketball player of all time? Many would say Michael Jordan. But Jordan won only six NBA championships; Bill Russell won eleven. Who's to say he is not the greatest?

Who is the greatest actor or actress of all time? Is it the one who won the most Oscars or the one who brought in the biggest box office receipts? The debate is endless.

What's missing is a clear consensus for how we define and measure "the Greatest of All Time" (the GOAT).

The way the world measures the GOAT may or may not line up with God's metrics for greatness.

A New Measure

We often think of greatness in terms of *accumulation* and *accomplishment*. The people we tend to call great are people who either *have* a lot or they've *done* a lot. We equate greatness with success. The measuring sticks we use are *how big, how much,* or *how many*. If that's the criteria, few of us would qualify for even the semifinals of becoming the GOAT.

I suspect, however, that there are many—maybe even you!—who could qualify for consideration. But I wouldn't use the world's definition; I would use *God's*. There's a difference between doing great things and being a great person.

On several occasions Jesus schooled his disciples, and schools us, about true greatness. If you have even a tablespoon of desire to be considered great in Christ's eyes, then you should know Jesus's secret to greatness. It's *service*.

The world measures greatness by how many people serve you. Jesus measures greatness by how many people you serve. The world measures greatness by who is in first place. Jesus measures greatness by who is in last place. The world measures greatness by those who get, but Jesus measures greatness by those who give. That's why I believe the way we serve others is by giving our lives away.

Approach Serving the Right Way

On one occasion, recorded for us in Matthew 20, the mother of James and John came to Jesus saying, "I want my boys to be on your All-Star Team. I want them to have top billing. I want them to have front-row seats. I want them to be great." If we're honest, she's not much different than we are. Everybody wants to be first: first in line, first to be chosen, first to be noticed, first to be praised. Every team in every sport wants to be the last one standing at the end of every season saying, "We're number one!"

When the other ten disciples heard about the brash inquiry, they were ticked off. And if you'd been Peter, Andrew, Philip, or one of the others, you would have been too! Suddenly everybody is jockeying for position. Everybody wants to be the GOAT.

But Jesus inverts the way they are approaching greatness, explaining, "But whoever would be great among you must be your servant" (Matthew 20:26).

Jesus turns greatness upside down and inside out.

If you purpose to seek greatness the Jesus way, be warned. If you choose to be more concerned about serving than being served, a war is going to break out in your mind and heart. It is a war between servanthood and self-centeredness.

Appreciate Serving the Right Way

There is nothing wrong with wanting to be first if you understand where first place is. Jesus explains to his friends, "If anyone would be first, he must be last of all and servant of all" (Mark 9:35).

You want to be number one? Then here is the secret: look for every opportunity you can to be number two. You want to be considered as one of the greatest of all time? Then learn this lesson: greatness starts at the bottom. You want to be like Jesus Christ? Find the least desired position. Find a job nobody else wants to do. Find the worst seat in the house.

I recently came across a nugget of wisdom, and though I have no idea who made it, I'd shake their hand and thank them if I did: "The basic trouble in the human situation is that people wish to do as little as possible and to get as much as possible. It is only when they are filled with the desire to put into life more than they take out that life for themselves and for others will be happy and prosperous."

To Jesus, greatness doesn't come from what you accumulate or accomplish. It comes from how much and how many you serve. The moment you choose to have a servant spirit, a servant heart, and a servant attitude, then our Creator says, "You are great."

Apply Serving the Right Way

Jesus spoke clearly: "You want to go to the front of the line? Get to the back of the line."

The mission statement at the church in Atlanta where I serve reads: "Love God, Serve Others, and Share Your Story." We invite and challenge and expect people to *serve*. Even those who aren't yet loving God by following Christ, even those who don't yet have that story of grace to share. We believe that anyone can serve others, both inside the church and outside. When someone wants to give their life away in service, we help them find opportunities to use their gifts to serve others at the point of their need.

Some of the greatest guys at my church are the ones who serve in the parking lot, through rain and snow and heat and hail. More great ones are the greeters at the door. Still other great ones are the people who, week in and week out, care for the babies in our church, the adults and teens who work in our children's and students' ministry, the guys up in the sound booth.

In Jesus's eyes and mine, they are the greatest.

Can you see the great ones around you?

This Week's Prayer: *Lord, give me a holy desire to be great in your kingdom by giving my life away to others and bearing witness to your greatness.*

This Week's Question: According to Jesus's new economy, who are the surprising great ones in your community?

46

A Servant First

This week's Scriptures:

- John 13:1-17
- Romans 12:3-8
- Mark 10:35-45

- Hebrews 6:9-12
- Galatians 5:13-15

A Surprising Reversal

Do you know why we enjoy a massage or a manicure or going to a plush resort or even to a restaurant to eat? We love to be served. We love to have other people wait on us.

But toward the end of his ministry, Jesus turns that natural human impulse upside down and inside out.

Outside of the crucifixion, John 13 offers possibly the single most amazing picture of the Son of God in any of the four Gospels. John describes Jesus doing something that no other self-respecting Jew or Gentile would do unless that person happened to be the lowest rung on the social ladder: a slave.

Jesus washes his friends' stinky feet!

There's actually far more to this story than washing dirty feet, because Jesus explains, "What I am doing you do not understand now, but afterward you will understand" (John 13:7). There is a deeper meaning and a deeper message, for Jesus's disciples and for us, because Jesus was not primarily dealing with a person's feet. He was talking about a person's *heart*.

More than anything else, Jesus desires two things from his followers: a surrendered heart and a servant spirit. We love being served, but Jesus had a totally different agenda. Jesus demonstrates that there is a far greater joy in serving than in *being* served.

See Opportunities

Jesus knows that he is God. Yet he prepares himself to wash his disciples' dirty, grimy, smelly, filthy feet and dry them off with a towel. He is willing to perform for his disciples a task that was so demeaning and degrading, the disciples wouldn't do it for him, much less for one another.

In the first century, people didn't wear shoes. They either went barefoot or wore sandals. They didn't have sidewalks and paved streets. Instead, they walked on dirt and mud. When guests would come to your home, they would take their sandals off at the door, and usually a servant would be there to wash their feet. And in a hired banquet room like this, an attendant would have been there to wash the feet. But at the Last Supper, evidently there was no servant to do this. So the disciples pinched their nose and held their breath and left their feet unwashed.

Why didn't any of these disciples see this need? Their problem was one we wrestle with in our time: they were focused on themselves; Jesus was focused on them. They were looking out for number one; he was looking out for numbers one through twelve.

They needed, and we need, to open our eyes. We need to see the hurt, the hopelessness, the helplessness, the heartache that is all around us as an opportunity to be used to touch and to change lives for the glory of Christ.

Serve Others

Do you know what these disciples were doing before Jesus washed their feet? Believe it or not, they were arguing about who was the greatest! They were so busy worrying and arguing over who would be top dog, who would be number one, who would get the best seat in the house, that they forgot about taking care of their dirty feet (Luke 22:24-30).

So Jesus takes off his outer garments, strips down to his undergarments, leaving his legs and upper body totally bare, takes a towel, and begins this unbelievably mundane, menial, almost humiliating task of washing feet. We have all heard of "throwing in the towel." In this case, Jesus was "picking up the towel."

To see the hands of the holy Son of God washing the dirty feet of sinful men? It's not right. The disciples ought to be washing his feet. But all the time they are arguing, the basin of water sits in the corner, the towel lies on the floor, and nobody is willing to lift a hand to help—except Jesus.

Unfortunately, some things never change.

Same Old, Same Old

We live in a world that is always asking, "How high are you in the company?" "How much money do you make?" "How many people report to you?"

At the same time, the Lord is asking, "How low are you?" "How many people are you serving?"

When it comes to serving people, you can't play favorites. Recall John 13:2: "During supper, when the devil had already put it into the heart of Judas Iscariot, Simon's son, to betray him," Jesus stooped down and served a man whose feet were caked with the dirt of disloyalty. Jesus served the betrayer in the same way he served the other disciples.

This doesn't come naturally. It's not natural to *not* look out for number one. What comes naturally is for us to say, "Every man for himself." What comes naturally is for us to say, "That is not my problem."

Jesus explains, "For I have given you an example, that you also should do just as I have done to you" (John 13:15).

Jesus was not telling us we ought to be literally washing feet. He was not establishing just another ritual to follow. He was saying *think the same way*.

Surrender Ourselves

Peter said to Jesus, "You shall never wash my feet." I think Jesus probably said, "Peter, you had better let me wash them, because you are about to put one in your mouth!" Jesus is about to do for Peter what Peter should have been doing for him. And when Peter tries to refuse, Jesus warns him, "If I do not wash you, you have no share with me" (John 13:8).

That obviously shook Peter to the core, because he goes from "you're not going to wash my feet" to "in that case, grab a rubber duck and we'll jump in the tub together!" Jesus explained that when you surrender your dirty life to him, he bathes you in his grace and in his love and in his forgiveness. You are in his eyes completely clean.

Peter's refusal seems like humility, but it was actually pride. Not only was Jesus doing for Peter what he should have been doing for Jesus, but Peter was also, in a sense, denying that his feet were dirty.

The good news of the Gospel is that once Jesus bathes you in the waters of his saving grace, you never need another bath. However, your feet will get dirty. Once we surrender ourselves to him and admit we need him to wash us, only then will we see the opportunities, every day, to follow his example and to serve the needs of others.

This Week's Prayer: *Lord, I thank you that you have cleansed me from head to toe. Teach me to humble myself, as you have, by serving others in your name.*

This Week's Question: In what ways is Jesus inviting you to "wash feet" this week?

47

The Victor

This week's Scriptures:

- Matthew 4:1-11
- James 4:6-8
- James 1:12-15

- 1 Corinthians 10:6-13
- Hebrews 2:14-18

Fight of the Century

I was a freshman in college on March 8, 1971, when "the fight of the century" took place. I was so excited and I could only get updates on the radio. It was the talk of the entire campus. For the first time in history, there was going to be a match between an unbeaten, former heavyweight boxing champion against the current, unbeaten heavyweight champion. Smokin' Joe Frazier was facing Mohammad Ali.

Frazier was 27 years old, 26 and 0 in his fights, with 23 knockouts. Ali was 29 years old, 31 and 0, with 25 knockouts. Neither fighter had ever lost.

Tickets were going for $150 a pop and the fight was watched by 300 million people around the world. Ali and Frasier were both guaranteed the unprecedented sum of $2.5 million dollars each.

I will never forget when the report came over the radio that Joe Frasier had defeated Mohammd Ali and had retained the heavy-weight championship of the world. People all over my dorm erupted, some happy, some angry, but nobody doubted that the fight had lived up to its billing.

But the fight of the ages played out two thousand years ago, described compellingly in Matthew 4:1-11. Considering its impact on human history, we might label it the definitive heavyweight championship of all time.

Fierce Competitors

In one corner was the devil himself. Most bookies would have made him the favorite for the fight. He was refreshed. He'd trained hard. He had all the backing of hell. He'd been planning his attack since the beginning of time, and he had inflicted at least one defeat on every opponent he had ever faced.

In the other corner was Jesus Christ. The underdog. He'd been out in the hot desert for forty days and he'd had nothing to eat. He was battling Satan and all the forces of hell, totally alone.

Satan throws three of his best punches against Jesus Christ, and if any one of them had landed, there would be no hope for you and no hope for me to spend eternity with God. If Satan had scored a knockout, none of us would have any hope of defeating sin in this life or in the life to come.

That's exactly why Matthew records this story.

It shows, without a doubt, that even though temptation is going to come to all of us, we can also know that temptation does not have to defeat any of us.

Don't Be Surprised by Temptation, Expect It

Many people confuse temptation with sin, but it is not a sin to be tempted. When someone is being tempted, it does not mean that they are living a substandard Christian life. It doesn't mean that they are out of the will of God. It doesn't mean that they are being disobedient.

Case in point: Jesus. Jesus was the Son of God. He was being led by the Spirit of God. He was totally submissive to the will of God, and he was totally under the power of God. And there was never a time in the life of Jesus Christ when he was closer to his Father than he was during these forty days in the wilderness.

Jesus was not just tempted as the Son of God, Jesus was tempted as the Son of Man. In his *humanity*, Jesus Christ had to face Satan just like you and I do.

The Bible says that the devil does not want what is best for you, he wants what is worst for you. If he can, he will tempt you to destroy your marriage. He will tempt you to throw your life away on alcohol and drugs. He will tempt you to give in, as David did, to that one-night stand. Don't be surprised by temptation; expect it.

Don't Be Fooled by Temptation, Detect It

The three specific ways that Satan tempted Jesus are the same three ways that Satan will tempt us.

For starters, we can expect temptation that will appeal to the *physical* (Matthew 4:2-3). After forty days of fasting, Jesus was ready for a double cheeseburger and a milk shake. This temptation goes all the way back to the Garden of Eden when Satan offered Eve the forbidden fruit. The great deceiver was asking Jesus—as with Eve—to substitute the physical for the spiritual.

In the second temptation, we learn to expect that temptation will appeal to the *emotional* (Matthew 4:5-6). The devil takes Jesus to the highest point in the city, to the southeast corner of the temple, overlooking the Kidron Valley. Satan says to Jesus, "Why don't you do a double backflip and a swan dive down below. You will become the talk of the town." That would feel good, wouldn't it? Each one of us has, at some time, gotten in trouble because rather than letting God's Word rule us, we let our feelings rule us.

We can also expect that temptation will appeal to the *spiritual* (Matthew 4:8-9). Satan offered the Lord Jesus exactly the same kingdoms as his heavenly Father was going to offer him, if he would just skip the cross. Satan wanted Jesus to be the shortcut Savior because Satan is the master of shortcuts.

We can detect the enemy's temptations as they appeal to the physical, the emotional, and the spiritual.

Don't Be Defeated by Temptation, Reject It

Jesus had two secret weapons to fight temptation. And they're the same ones we have. Jesus was filled with the Spirit and he was armed with the Scriptures.

Jesus was led by the Holy Spirit of God. He was, and we are, *led* only as we *follow*. We follow someone only if we are totally surrendered and submitted to their authority. We surrender our lives to the Holy

Spirit because he is God's nuclear weapon that will enable us to defeat temptation.

Jesus Christ was also armed with the Scriptures. Jesus never tried to argue with the devil; he didn't try to negotiate with the devil; he never tried to debate with the devil. He didn't use magic formulas or magic words. He didn't use holy water or anointed handkerchiefs. He used the Word of God.

Years and years ago, the Yellow Pages used the slogan, "Let your fingers do the walking." When it comes to temptation, there is one piece of advice to follow: let the Word of God do the talking. When you do, James 4:7 will be realized in your life: "Submit yourselves therefore to God. Resist the devil, and he will flee from you."

This Week's Prayer: *Lord, I trust that you've prepared me to fight the good fight. Fill me with your Spirit and gird me with your Word to resist the temptations of the enemy.*

This Week's Question: As you think of the recurring temptations in your life, are they aimed at the physical, the emotional, or the spiritual?

48

Commander in Chief

This week's Scriptures:

- Luke 9:23-27
- Ephesians 5:1-2
- 2 Corinthians 5:11-15
- Romans 14:5-9
- 1 Peter 2:19-23

Are You All In?

I have never played poker, but poker has always fascinated me. Have you ever noticed that in poker games in movies, and especially in the old Westerns, the most dramatic scenes are when somebody puts all his chips on the table? When a player does that, he is saying to all the other players, "I'm betting everything I have. I'm committing all that I've got."

The term "bet the ranch" came from the Wild West. If a gambler thought he had a shot at the big pot, he might put the deed to the ranch on the table and bet the ranch that he had a winning hand. Or he could take a piece of paper, sign his own handmade promissory note, and bet everything he had on that particular hand. Poker players call it "going all in."

Though he wasn't a gambler, Jesus loved going all in.

Living Wholehearted

The most nervous I've ever been—more than speaking to twenty-five thousand people, more than being in the Oval Office with the president of the United States—was the five minutes before I got married. Waiting to walk into the church with the pastor, I realized that I was about to commit my life to a woman I had known for only six months. I was pacing back and forth, sweating bullets and hyperventilating.

This wasn't a contract that could be declared null and void with thirty days' notice; we were making a covenant before God that would be until death do us part. When the pastor asks, "Will you take this woman for better or for worse, for richer or for poorer, in sickness or in health?" it's not multiple choice! Marriage is a commitment when it's good or bad, when you're happy or angry. Marriage is 'til death do you part.

That's *all in.*

When God sent Jesus Christ to this world, he went all in. When Jesus went to the cross to die for our sins, he went all in. The wholehearted Lord is not interested in halfhearted followers. He is looking for people who are all in.

Deny Yourself

Many choose not to follow Jesus because of the requirement he gives that we deny ourselves (Luke 9:23). Jesus is honest as he explains, "There is a cost to following me. You've got to deny the hardest thing to deny, which is yourself."

One Sunday I surprised my congregation by announcing, publicly, the church member who was giving me the most problems. Seriously, this guy was my biggest headache. I wasn't sure if I should say his name out loud because—at one level—I liked the guy. I loved being around him, and he's one of the best people I know. With a bit of fear and trepidation, I said aloud that the church member who was giving me the most trouble was...*me*! I have to constantly tell myself to get out of the way so Jesus can have his way.

Jesus said, "If you are going to follow me, step one is to deny yourself." That means you have to put Jesus before you, above you, ahead of you, and instead of you. You've got to get the makeup of your life to be all of Jesus and none of you.

Die to Yourself

In a scene from the movie *Act of Valor*, a Navy Seal is about to leave his wife and newborn baby to go to war. The commanding officer is asking this soldier if he is ready to make this sacrifice. The soldier replies, "If you haven't given up everything, you have already lost."

Similarly, Jesus speaks plainly, "If anyone would come after me, let him deny himself and take up his cross daily and follow me. For whoever would save his life will lose it, but whoever loses his life for my sake will save it" (Luke 9:23-24).

A few years ago, a doctor came to the parents of conjoined twins and said, "If I do not perform surgery quickly to separate these twins, both of them are going to die."

"You obviously have our permission," the parents replied. "Begin immediately."

"You don't understand," he said. "It's not that simple. I can save one, but I can't save the other. I can save either, but I can't save both. What I'm telling you is the two of you must make a decision on which one is going to live and which one is going to die."

Jesus asks you to make a similar choice. If Jesus is going to live in you, you must die to you. Jesus said it is only when you have given up everything for him that you are ready to gain everything from him that you are ready to "follow him."

Devote Yourself

Are you all in? Have you bet the ranch on Jesus Christ?

If you're single, are you all in when it comes to your sexual purity and your holiness? All in concerning what you see and what you hear?

How about marriage? Have you bet the ranch? Do you need to say to your spouse all over again, "I am *all in* with this relationship, and no matter what else happens, it's going to be 'til death do us part"?

Are you all in with your money? Are all your chips on the table when it comes to doing Christ's work? That is what following Jesus means.

Jesus's call, first to his disciples and today to us, is to be *all in*.

You may remember studying the explorer Hernando Cortés in school. He was from Spain, and in 1519 he came to Mexico and landed at Veracruz. He had been given orders to conquer the land and to build a colony. When all of his men were off the boats, he did something for which he has been remembered for almost five hundred years. He burned all his boats. He looked at his men and said, "We will either win this victory or we will die, but we are not going back."

Do you know what he did? He bet the ranch. He was all in. There is only one way to follow Jesus Christ: burn the boats, bet the ranch, and go all in.

This Week's Prayer: *Lord, because of the work and witness of Jesus Christ, I'm convinced that you are worth betting the ranch on. Give me courage, this week, to be* all in.

This Week's Question: Is there an area of your life where you've held back? What chips of yours need to be on the table?

Jesus, the Overcomer

What separates Jesus from every other human and religious figure in history was not what he did *during* his life but what he accomplished in his final hours. More than his miracles or parables, teachings or maxims, Jesus is defined by the way he overcame death for the sake of humankind. In Jesus's last days, he overcame the three greatest problems of life—sin, sorrow, and death—and through this, he gives us hope that we can also be victorious when our life's final chapter has been written.

49

The Passion of the Christ—
the Rest of the Story

This week's Scriptures:

- Matthew 27:1-10,27-31
- Isaiah 53:1-6
- Psalm 22

- Romans 5:6-11
- 1 Peter 3:13-18

Cause for Passion

In 2004, a frequent question being asked in the United States was, "Have you seen *The Passion of the Christ*?" If the answer was no, the next question was, "Are you going to see it?" If the answer was yes, the next question was, "What did you think about it?"

Mel Gibson's movie—produced entirely in Aramaic and Latin, using subtitles—was a huge Hollywood blockbuster grossing more than six-hundred-million dollars during its theatrical release, making it the highest grossing non-English-language film of all time.

The Passion is the story of one-half of one day of one man's life. So why is this day different from all others? Why did millions of people have such passion about *The Passion*?

The response of one Roman soldier gives us a clue.

A centurion and some of his guards, who'd coldly witnessed and executed thousands of crucifixions without batting an eye, make a startling confession, "Truly this was the Son of God!" (Matthew 27:54).

This film was impactful because it recounted twelve hours of the life of *Christ*. If Jesus was just another man, then this was just another death. But if Jesus was more than a man, if he *was* the Son of God, then there has never been another death like his.

Who Was the Christ?

The premise behind forensic fingerprint evidence is that each individual has unique ridges on his or her fingers. When a print is found on an object that matches the pattern of ridges on a person's finger, you can conclude with scientific certainty that the individual has touched that object.

A set of prophetic fingerprints in the Old Testament establishes to an unbelievable degree of certainty that Jesus was the Son of God and the Messiah.

Isaiah announces, "Behold, the virgin shall conceive and bear a son, and shall call his name Immanuel" (Isaiah 7:14). And Matthew 1:18-25 confirms that Jesus was indeed born of the virgin Mary.

Micah 5:2 says the Messiah would hail from Bethlehem, and Luke 2:1-7 tells us that Jesus was indeed born in Bethlehem.

Zechariah 11:12-13 predicted the price of the betrayal would be thirty pieces of silver. Matthew 26:15 and 27:3-10 corroborate that he was betrayed for thirty pieces of silver.

Psalm 22:16 predicted that the Messiah's hands and feet would be pierced, which they were at his crucifixion. This prophecy was given seven hundred years before crucifixion had even been employed!

These are just a few of over three hundred prophecies Jesus fulfilled. The overwhelming evidence is that Jesus was the Messiah, the Son of God.

How Did He Die?

You can't appreciate *why* Jesus died unless you understand *how* he died.

Before every Roman execution, the victim was stripped naked, tied to a flogging post, and scourged. The instrument was a short whip called a *flagrum*, made of two or three leather thongs. These thongs were braided with pieces of sheep bone, metal, and iron attached at various intervals. The back, the buttocks, and the legs were flogged, and with each blow, flesh would be torn away exposing the muscles, until the entire backside of the victim was nothing but quivering ribbons of bleeding flesh. In other words, Jesus was already in critical condition before he was even nailed to the cross.

For the crucifixion itself, the victim was laid on a crossbeam, then spikes that were five inches long and tapered to a razor-sharp point were driven through the wrist of both arms. Then the feet would have been fixed to the cross and seven-inch spikes would have been driven through both feet. Once the cross was in the upright position, the victim would die a slow death by asphyxiation.

What finally caused the death of Jesus Christ? Doctors would say take your pick: hypovolemic shock, exhaustion, asphyxiation, dehydration, arrhythmia or congestive heart failure.[15] The word *excruciating* comes from the Latin word meaning "from the cross."

Why Did He Die?

Why would the Messiah, the Son of God, have to die such a violent, terrible, excruciating death? The Scripture is plain. First, he died for sin. Isaiah says,

> We're all like sheep who've wandered off and gotten lost.
>   We've all done our own thing, gone our own way.
> And GOD has piled all our sins, everything we've done wrong,
>   on him, on him.
>
> (Isaiah 53:6 MSG)

Peter also confirms,

> He personally carried our sins
>   in his body on the cross
> so that we can be dead to sin
>   and live for what is right.
> By his wounds
>   you are healed.
>
> (1 Peter 2:24 NLT)

Yet for Jesus, more awful than the pain of physical suffering he endured was the spiritual pain of bearing the guilt for our sins. He died not only for sin; he died *in place of* the sinner.

Romans 5:6 (NLT) announces, "When we were utterly helpless, Christ came at just the right time and died for us sinners." And 1 Peter 3:18 concurs, "For Christ also suffered once for sins, the righteous for the unrighteous, to bring you to God."

Jesus took on the cross what you will have to take for all eternity *if* you don't take Jesus. He died such a violent death to illustrate how horrible sin is, how holy God is, and how much we need him to die in our place for our sins.

What Am I to Do?

No serious historian doubts that a man named Jesus Christ lived, that his life impacted history, and that he was crucified on a Roman cross outside of Jerusalem around AD 30. But Christianity claims that Jesus not only died but that he was raised from the dead, which is how the movie ends.

For two thousand years, no one has tried to refute that the tomb was empty, even though it caused a great uproar in Palestine. An ancient decree of Claudius Caesar, who reigned from AD 41–54, was discovered in Nazareth that reads, "It is my pleasure that graves and tombs remain perpetually undisturbed...in case of violation I desire that the offender be sentenced to capital punishment on charge of violation of sepulchre."[16] Historians believe that the unusual step decreeing the death penalty for robbing a grave was a reaction to the uproar caused by the empty tomb of Jesus Christ.

That tomb has been empty for two thousand years, which is why the British historian Arnold Toynbee said, "If the body of one Jew, Jesus of Nazareth, can be produced, then Christianity will crumble into a lifeless religion." He was right. But they won't find the body, because he has risen from the dead.

Without the last two minutes of *The Passion*, it's just another movie about another man who lived and died just like billions of other people in history. But the crucified Christ of the first two hours and five minutes of that movie is the risen Lord of the last two minutes of that movie. Only God could come back from the grave. Whether you will receive him is up to you: you will determine the rest of the story.

This Week's Prayer: *Lord, pierce my heart with the reality of the suffering that pierced your body. And teach me how to live faithfully in response to your amazing love.*

This Week's Question: How does Jesus's suffering impact the relationship you have with him?

50

His Grace, My Place

This week's Scriptures:

- Matthew 27:11-26
- Hebrews 10:1-10
- Galatians 3:10-14
- 1 John 4:7-12
- Titus 3:3-7

A Compelling Question

We're familiar with capital punishment in the United States. In the past, we have used everything from the firing squad and the hangman's noose to the electric chair and the gas chamber. Today, in those rare cases where capital punishment is carried out, lethal injection has become the method of choice. Yet crucifixion is arguably the most painful and torturous death ever devised.

Today, American executions are private. Cameras are not allowed to capture any execution and usually only friends and family members are allowed to witness the event. In contrast, crucifixion in the Roman Empire was not only a public event, but the government actually wanted people to see a crucifixion to impress upon them the consequences for crossing the government's authority.

Furthermore, today's executions are swift and as much as possible humane. Death is generally brought on as quickly and quietly as possible. On the other hand, crucifixion was designed to be painful, humiliating, and lingering—sometimes lasting as long as nine days.

But Why?

The emphasis of the New Testament concerning Jesus Christ is not on his birth, nor his life, but on his death.

The apostle Paul wrote half of the New Testament, and yet if you read any of the books that he wrote, virtually the entire life and ministry of Jesus Christ is ignored. Paul seldom mentions Jesus's teachings. He never mentions his miracles. He never mentions the parables that he told. The emphasis is almost solely and singularly upon Christ's suffering and death and resurrection.

The death of Jesus Christ is emphasized because the death of Jesus Christ, along with his resurrection, was the singular act and event of his entire life. Every other person was born for the specific purpose of living. Jesus was born for the specific purpose of dying.

I'm amazed at how many people, even committed followers of Christ, have never considered *why* Jesus died. We know where, when, and how, but rarely do we ask *why*.

As we witness Jesus on the cross, we're reminded that he has come a long way from Bethlehem to Jerusalem. A long way from the manger to the cross. A long way from diapers to death. A long way from being a beautiful baby to being a condemned criminal. And in the back of our minds, we wonder *why?*

Jesus Sacrificed His Life for Me

The night before his crucifixion, Jesus's disciples had celebrated the Passover with him, remembering Israel's captivity in the nation of Egypt. God was going to free them from four hundred years of slavery to begin their journey to the Promised Land.

On the night that God was going to free them, God sent an angel over all of Egypt, and his job was to go to every home in Egypt and kill every firstborn child, which would force Pharaoh to let Israel go. The only way of escape was to kill a lamb and paint the blood over the doorpost. When the angel would see the blood, he would "pass over" the house and everyone would be safe. From that time until this day, Jews still celebrate the Passover.

Later, God instituted a formal system of animal sacrifice so that sacrifice and blood might cover sin. A person could bring a lamb to a priest and have that priest slay that lamb and take the blood of that lamb as a symbolic covering for that person's sins. This, however, was never meant to be a final remedy for sin but a temporary arrangement because "it is impossible for the blood of bulls and goats to take away sins" (Hebrews 10:4).

There was only *One* who could, once and for all, remove the world's sin. John the Baptist called him, called Jesus, "the lamb of God who takes away the sins of the world." Jesus is our Passover Lamb.

Jesus Substituted His Death for Me

When the crowd at Jesus's crucifixion was given the choice to release one prisoner—as was the local custom—they chose a notorious prisoner named Barabbas over Jesus (Matthew 27:15-26).

Barabbas was Osama bin Laden and Saddam Hussein rolled into one. He was a murderer, a robber, a rebel, and a thief who'd been convicted more than once, and he expected that this was the day he was going to die. I imagine that when he was set free from that prison, he wandered over to that place where he was supposed to be hanging. Maybe he even stood at the foot of that cross and mused, "I don't know who you are, but one thing I do know—you are dying in my place."

We are all Barabbas.

Jesus was not only Barabbas's substitute, he was *our* substitute. He not only died in his place, he died in *our* place. Paul later explains to the church in Galatia, "Christ...changed places with us and put himself under that curse" (Galatians 3:13 NCV).

In *The Passion of the Christ*, the hand holding the nail to be driven through the hand of Jesus is Mel Gibson's. This is the only role Gibson played in his own movie.

"I'm first in line for crucifying Jesus," Gibson explained. "I did it."

Mel Gibson, for all his other public and private flaws, seemed to understand that Jesus substituted his death for all of humanity.

Jesus Satisfied God's Justice for Me

When something is "atoned," it is paid for. Something is satisfied or a debt is taken care of. And what's satisfied in Jesus's atonement for our sins is the justice of God.

This may sound surprising, but the cross was not primarily for *us*. The cross was primarily for God the Father. Since the blood of animals was merely a credit payment, and only symbolic, Christ died to make that final and full payment to satisfy the justice of God. He did for us exactly what he did for Barabbas.

Before you and I were even born, before this world was even created, God the Father, God the Son, and God the Holy Spirit agreed that Jesus would take our punishment so that God could acquit us and still be justified in doing so.

As the world poured out its wrath upon Jesus Christ, at his trial and at his death, God's wrath against our sin was completely released upon Christ at the cross. The cross was all about three words: mercy, justice, grace. God's mercy deferred payment for sin. God's justice demanded payment for sin. God's grace delivered payment for sin.

This Week's Prayer: *Lord, make me a vessel of your mercy, justice, and grace by inviting others to meet you at the cross of Christ.*

This Week's Question: What meaning does Christ's great sacrifice have for your daily living? Does it make a difference?

51

The Warrior Rises

This week's Scriptures:

- Matthew 27:32-54
- Genesis 3:14-15
- Romans 3:21-26

- Luke 24:13-27
- John 20:1-10

Waiting for the Bruiser

As a kid, I would watch pro wrestling religiously on television every Saturday afternoon. The first wrestler I remember seeing was Dick "the Bruiser." I remember thinking as a kid that he was the ugliest, scariest man I had ever seen in my life. He was the dirtiest wrestler on television and went ten years without anyone pinning his shoulders to the mat. They called him "the Bruiser" because every opponent he ever fought he made sure they were left both bloodied and bruised.

For thousands of years, the nation of Israel had been looking for another bruiser. They weren't looking for a wrestler; they were looking for a warrior. They expected him to be a bruiser because he was predicted to be one. When Satan caused the world's greatest tragedy by successfully tempting Adam and Even to sin, war broke out between good and evil and between God and Satan. The only hope for this world was a warrior who could come and fight this war and defeat this enemy. He would do it by being a bruiser, as we read in Genesis,

> "I will put enmity between you and the woman,
>   and between your offspring and her offspring;
> he shall bruise your head,
>   and you shall bruise his heel."

> (Genesis 3:15)

237

From that lone prophecy, the picture of a warrior began to form in the minds and hearts of Israel's rabbis and scholars.

An Unexpected Hero

They expected this warrior to take over the world and usher in a kingdom where Israel would be restored to its rightful place as the dominant nation on the planet. No one would be able to touch him. No one would pin his shoulders to the mat. No one could hurt him, because he was the warrior, the bruiser.

God did send this warrior, his Son, to finish a war he didn't start. However, this warrior would not finish the war by killing but rather by dying. When you understand why Jesus died on the cross and what happened after his death on the cross, then you understand why only he could be the warrior who could give every one of us the ability to win our war over the two greatest problems this world faces: sin and death. Jesus is the only warrior who could defeat and who did defeat sin and death.

It's hard for us to imagine the shock, the bewilderment, and the dismay in the hearts of everyone who'd believed the warrior had finally arrived when Jesus is handed over to be crucified.

How could this be? Surely this warrior had not come to die without firing a shot, without throwing a spear, without shooting an arrow, or without wielding a sword. He lays his life down and dies? Suddenly many who had believed were wondering, "Could Jesus really have been God's warrior?"

Jesus Sacrificed His Life for Me

Much of this world does not take Jesus Christ seriously because they don't understand *why* he died. Most of us know *where* Jesus died: outside the city of Jerusalem. Most of us know *when* he died: roughly around AD 30. Most of us know *how* he died: by crucifixion. But pause to consider *why* he died.

As we discussed last week, the Passover was the first time that the blood of animals, painted over the door frames of Hebrew homes, was used to spare the lives of God's people. When the death angel that God sent would see the blood, he would "pass over" the house and everyone inside would be safe. God would later institute a formal system of animal sacrifice to cover sin.

Sin was an enemy too big for anybody to fight. It was a war too great for anybody to win—until the warrior came. This warrior used the only weapon that could defeat sin and death and bruise the devil, who caused it all. Though the people did not realize it yet, that weapon was not a sword or a spear or an arrow. It was a cross. This warrior performed the ultimate act any soldier can: he gave his life for the freedom of others.

Jesus Substituted His Death for Me

That God allowed his own Son to be that warrior and lay down his life for humanity means that you are in a war you can't win. Because of sin, you are in a battle and face an enemy called "death" that will kill you for all eternity if you do not put your faith and your trust in the warrior.

The apostle Paul explains, "whom God displayed publicly as a propitiation in His blood through faith. This was to demonstrate His righteousness, because in the forbearance of God He passed over the sins previously committed" (Romans 3:25 NASB).

Paul is referring to the time before Christ when animals were sacrificed as a credit charge for our sins. It wasn't payment, but rather a symbolic way of letting everyone know that payment was coming.

When it comes to sin, God's justice demands that someone pay the price. God can't just let bygones be bygones. Before you and I were even born, God the Son agreed to become the warrior who would take the sin of the human race upon himself. He would take our punishment. He would pay the bill. He would fight the battle. He would win the war, so that God could forgive us.

Jesus Satisfied God's Justice for Me

All of the wrath and punishment and judgment that your sin and my sin deserves, God put on this warrior who didn't come to kill, but who came to die. Who came not with a sword in one hand and a spear in the other, but who came with love on the one hand and grace on the other.

How do I know he was the warrior that was promised in the book of Genesis? Because everybody dies, how do I know this warrior was victorious just by his death? Many warriors have come, many warriors have fought, many warriors have bled, and many warriors have died. But the one surefire proof that he is that warrior is that the warrior rises!

You cannot go to heaven by being a good person; you will never be good enough. You cannot earn your way to heaven by being religious; you will never be religious enough. You cannot pay your way to heaven; there's not money enough. God doesn't grade on the curve but on the cross. And not just any cross, but the cross of the warrior who rises.

This Week's Prayer: *God, thank you for sending the warrior who dies and rises to free the ones you love from the grip of sin and death.*

This Week's Question: Are you truly convinced that your goodness cannot earn your ticket to heaven? Are you trusting completely in the cross of Jesus?

52

Dead Man Walking

This week's Scriptures:

- Matthew 27:57–28:10
- John 11:1-44
- Ecclesiastes 8:8
- Psalm 89:46-48
- Revelation 20:4-6

Hope for the Hopeless

In 1927 near Cape Cod, an S-4 Navy submarine was accidentally rammed by a Coast Guard cutter, sending it immediately to the bottom of the bay. The entire crew was trapped. Every effort was made to rescue them, but every effort failed. Near the end of the four-day attempt to bring these men to the surface, a diver placed his helmeted ear to the side of the vessel and heard a man tapping Morse code from inside. This was the last question he heard: "Is…there…any…hope?"[17]

Jesus is the only person in human history who answers this question. Because Christ has faced and overcome death, he gives hope to all of us. And not just the hope that there is life after death, but also that there is life after life—that is, Jesus proved there is more to life than just *this* life. Much more!

Everyone needs hope.

We need hope that our life matters today, but we also need hope that there is more to life than this life tomorrow. Everybody wants to know that they matter. We want to know that our life makes a difference here on earth and that somehow life continues after our journey on earth is over.

Every human being on this planet longs for significance and security.

Nobody knows that better than the God who made us, which is why he sent Jesus.

The Secret to Security

As we saw in section two of this book, John's Gospel records seven "I am" statements Jesus uses to explain to us who he is:

- "I am the resurrection and the life."
- "I am the good shepherd."
- "I am the bread of life."
- "I am the door."
- "I am the vine."
- "I am the light of the world."
- "I am the way, the truth, and the life."

Believe it or not, in these sayings is the secret to significance and security. Jesus is telling us through these tremendous truths that true significance and lasting security can be found only in him. All that we hope for, all that we need, can be found in him.

Knowing how we long for hope, knowing how we fear death, Jesus offered his followers, and offers us, a glimpse of what lies beyond this life for those who trust in him.

We get a peek into Jesus's victory over death when John 11 describes the most famous funeral in history. It took place in a little village called Bethany for a man named Lazarus. (We looked earlier, back in chapter 8, at this event, but we have more to glean from this important story, so stay with me here.)

Lazarus wasn't an important man in his community, and yet what Jesus said and did for Lazarus forever drains death of its dread and empties the future of fear.

We Must Expect the Fact of Death

As we noted previously, Jesus often stayed in Bethany with Lazarus and his sisters, Mary and Martha, whenever he would come to Jerusalem.

They were the best of friends. When Lazarus became extremely ill, the sisters sent word to Jesus that he was sick, thinking he would come immediately and rectify the situation. Instead, Jesus deliberately delayed going to make sure that Lazarus did indeed die. Yes, even Jesus's best friends die.

To the degree that it's in our power, most of us do all we can to avoid death. We buckle up, drive cars equipped with air bags, sleep more, run farther, eat less fat, consume more protein, drink less caffeine, crunch more vegetables, take our vitamins, hit the gym, and much more.

Yet the Greek poet Euripides noted, "Death is the debt we all must pay." Though it is closer for some than others, death is inevitable. It might be delayed, but never avoided. Ecclesiastes 8:8 (NLT) says,

> None of us can hold back our spirit from departing. None of us has the power to prevent the day of our death. There is no escaping that obligation, that dark battle.

And the psalmist concurs,

> No one can live forever; all will die.
> No one can escape the power of the grave.
> (Psalm 89:48 NLT)

We Will Experience the Force of Death

When Jesus finally made his way to Bethany, Martha was not real thrilled to see him. In a curt fashion, she said, "Lord, if you had been here, my brother would not have died" (John 11:21.)

Words like that have been echoed a million times down through history: "If you had been here, my baby would have lived," or "If you had been here, my marriage would not have ended."

I spoke at a businessmen's luncheon recently about what the Bible means when it says that God works everything out for the good of those who love him. A young man came up to me afterward when I was all alone, looked around to make sure that nobody could hear him, and with tears in his eyes said, "You preached that message for me."

I said, "What do you mean?"

He told me how two years earlier, his two-and-a-half-year-old son drowned in a swimming pool. He had gone to a party where all four of his older children were in the pool along with about twelve other people, but no one saw the little boy go under, and he died.

This grieving father needed to hear that the presence of death does not mean the absence of God.

After hearing Martha out, Jesus spoke into her confusion and ours:

> "I am the resurrection and the life. Whoever believes in me, though he die, yet shall he live, and everyone who lives and believes in me shall never die. Do you believe this?" (John 11:25-26).

We Can Escape the Fear of Death

Moving to the tomb, calling on God to answer his prayer, Jesus shouts out three words that sent chills up the spines of everyone standing around that tomb:

> "Lazarus, come out" (John 11:43).

You could have heard a pin drop.

Everybody was staring in amazement. Lazarus had now been dead four days. When a person died, they would wrap the body in spices and then tape him up like a mummy. Everybody was trying to figure out what in the world Jesus was doing.

Then, Lazarus came out.

Jesus not only liberated Lazarus from the bonds of death, he liberated Lazarus from the fear of death. People came from miles around to see the man who had been raised from the dead, and he told them what Jesus had done for him. Later, the Pharisees wanted to kill him. But do you think Lazarus was worried about their plan? Do you think he was afraid of dying?

They threatened him, "If you don't quit witnessing for Christ, you are going to die."

Lazarus replied, "Been there. Done that. No big deal."

The One who performed that unforgettable miracle on Lazarus later went to the cross, hung there, and died, paying the complete penalty for your sin and mine. He, too, was wrapped in burial cloths. He, too, was placed in the grave. He, too, was sealed with a stone. But three days later he was alive, never to die again.

We must answer Jesus's query to Martha: *Do you believe this?*

I hope you do because there's nobody like Jesus. Never has been. Never will be.

This Week's Prayer: *Lord, I thank you that in your dying and rising, you have become hope for the hopeless. I praise you for being—for me and for the world—the resurrection and the life!*

This Week's Question: Do you believe, in your deep places, that those who believe in Jesus will never die?

Acknowledgments

I plan my preaching out a year in advance, and in 2013 our church spent a year with Jesus. Every message for fifty-two weeks came only from the four Gospels—Matthew, Mark, Luke, and John. Not coincidentally, we had the greatest year in the life of our young church in every meaningful metric you could imagine. Our church grew leaps and bounds spiritually right before my very eyes.

It was with a similar hope and thought in mind that this book was born. Having a book at one's fingertips that could instantly take you back two millennia to listen to this one of a kind God-man speak life-changing truth into your heart was the goal. There are several who helped me along the way.

Margot Starbuck took some rough clay and, with her magical hands, molded it into material that is eminently reader friendly and pleasant to the ear.

My son Jonathan, an unbelievably gifted writer himself, was an invaluable resource in suggestions, editions, revisions, and most of all encouragement to even get back into the publishing game.

Rod Morris, my editor at Harvest House, is unparalleled at smoothing rough edges no one else but his eyes can see.

Robert and Eric Wolgemuth are both friends and advocates whose guidance and representation have been most appreciated.

My church, Cross Pointe, is just a joy to pastor and preach to. Thanks for letting me be your shepherd!

My treasured wife of almost four decades, Teresa, is always by my side as a Proverbs 31 wife, freeing me to do things like write this book. She is just the best!

It is always a joy to work with the wonderful folks at Harvest House so ably led by my dear friend Bob Hawkins. Thanks for letting me be part of the team.

Finally, I must say it again. There is *nobody* like Jesus. Never has been and never will be (John 14:6).

About the Author

James Merritt is senior pastor of Cross Pointe Church in Duluth, Georgia, and the host of *Touching Lives*, a television show that broadcasts weekly in all 50 states and 122 countries. He formerly served as a two-term president of the Southern Baptist Convention, America's largest Protestant denomination. As a national voice on faith and leadership, he has been interviewed by *Time*, *Fox News*, *ABC World News*, *MSNBC*, and *60 Minutes*.

He is author of nine books, including *How to Impact and Influence Others: 9 Keys to Successful Leadership*; *What God Wants Every Dad to Know*; and *Still Standing: 8 Winning Strategies for Facing Tough Times*.

Dr. Merritt holds a bachelor's degree from Stetson University and a master's and doctor of philosophy from Southern Baptist Theological Seminary. He and his wife, Teresa, reside outside of Atlanta near their three children and two grandchildren.

Follow him on Twitter at @DrJamesMerritt.

Notes

1. Jaroslav Pelikan, *Jesus Through the Centuries: His Place in the History of Culture* (New Haven, CT: Yale University Press, 1985), 1.

2. Tim Stafford, *Surprised by Jesus: His Agenda for Changing Everything in A.D. 30 and Today* (Downers Grove, IL: InterVarsity Press, 2006), 10.

3. Matt Crenson, "Genealogists Discover Royal Roots for All," *NBC News.com*, July 1, 2006, www.msnbc.msn.com/id/13662242.

4. James C. Coleman, *Abnormal Psychology in Modern Life* (Glenview, IL: Scott, Foresman and Co., 1964), 72, 160.

5. Rudolf Bultmann, *Kerygma and Myth* (San Francisco: Harper, 1961), 4-5.

6. www.cuttingedge.org/News/n2246.cfm.

7. Raymond McHenry, "You Are God's Stradivarius," *McHenry's Stories for the Soul* (Peabody, MA: Hendrickson Publishers, 2001), 290.

8. David Kinnaman and Gabe Lyons, *UnChristian* (Grand Rapids, MI: Baker Books, 2007), 182, 187.

9. *Leadership Journal* (Winter 1983), 43.

10. George H. Gallup Jr., *Religion in America* (Princeton, NJ: Princeton Religion Research Center, 1996), 4, 12, 19.

11. Philip Yancey, *Prayer* (Grand Rapids, MI: Zondervan, 2006), 13.

12. Caitlin Flannigan, "Why Marriage Matters," *Time*, July 13, 2009, 47.

13. Cited in Kinnaman and Lyons, *UnChristian*, 198.

14. Perhaps in your Bible you notice brackets around this passage of Scripture with a footnote stating this story is not found in some of the oldest available New Testament manuscripts. Without going into great detail, many scholars believe that this story not only has strong manuscript support, but rings true to what we know about Jesus. It also fits the context of what comes before it and what comes after it.

15. *CJAMA*, March 21, 1986, vol. 255, 11.

16. Cited in John R.W. Stott, *The Cross of Christ* (Downers Grove, IL: InterVarsity Press, 1986).

17. "Coast Guard Cutter Collides with Navy Submarine," http://massmoments.org; Ben Patterson, *The Grand Essentials* (Waco, TX: Word Books, 1987), 35.

Also by James Merritt

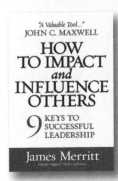

How to Impact and Influence Others
9 Keys to Successful Leadership

A person's character—who he is—determines the impact he has on others. James Merritt, senior pastor of Cross Pointe Church and host of the television program *Touching Lives*, unlocks nine key character qualities that, if consistently exercised and seen by others, will influence them to reach their full potential.

Readers of this book will be motivated to leave a lasting impact in a number of ways, such as

- making sure someone sees, hears, or feels love from them each day
- letting God's joy shine through their life
- being kind to someone every day
- being faithful and dependable
- treating others as more important

No one can do anything about his heritage, but he can do something about his legacy. Beginning today, he can become the kind of person who makes a life-changing difference for others, perhaps even an *eternal* difference. *How to Impact and Influence Others* shows the way to a life of surpassing influence.

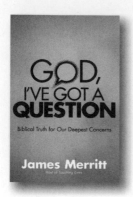

God, I've Got a Question
Biblical Truth for Our Deepest Concerns

James Merritt, popular pastor, author, and host of the television show *Touching Lives*, knows that when people wrestle with doubts, they are missing out on the security, promises, and power of Christ.

Avoiding academic lingo, Merritt presents relatable, relevant responses to the hard questions that seekers and Christians hesitate to ask or answer:

- Why is there so much suffering in the world if God is in control?
- How can I discover God's will for my life?
- Why is Jesus the only way to God, and how can I defend this?
- What should I do about the moral gray areas of my life?
- Why should anybody believe the Bible?

Whether read straight through or used as a reference for specific topics, this insightful resource reveals the uncompromised truths of the Christian faith and the depth and importance of its precepts for every person, every life.

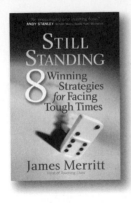

Still Standing
8 Winning Strategies for Facing Tough Times

Everybody faces tough times. No one gets a free pass from those make-or-break moments that lead to character development, achievement, and fulfillment.

The Bible is replete with stories of people who faced tough times and stood firm in their faith. From these stories, James Merritt uncovers guiding principles and winning strategies to help us face our own challenges and find victory in the midst of adversity. Examples include:

- Joseph, who illustrates how to respond when we get what we don't deserve
- Daniel, who inspires us to stand for what's right when no one else does or will
- Esther, who emboldens us to place the well-being of others above our own comfort and security

When life threatens to trip us up, push us over, or knock us down, we *can* stand tall. *Still Standing* points the way toward a life of freedom, joy, and victory as we discover God's winning strategies for tackling tough times head-on.

To learn more about Harvest House books and
to read sample chapters, visit our website:

www.harvesthousepublishers.com

HARVEST HOUSE PUBLISHERS
EUGENE, OREGON